MANY MOUNTAINS TO CLIMB

Reflections on Competence, Courage, and Commitment

Stacy Allison

BookPartners
Wilsonville, Oregon

Portions of the text of this book were co-authored by Peter Carlin and were originally published in *Beyond the Limits: A Woman's Triumph on Everest* (Little, Brown, 1993).

Library of Congress Cataloging-in-Publication Data

Allison, Stacy.
   Many mountains to climb : reflections on competence, courage, and commitment / Stacy Allison.
       p.   cm.
   ISBN 1-58151-011-X (trade pbk. : alk. paper)
   1. Mountaineering. 2. Mountaineering--Everest, Mount (China and Nepal)   I. Title
GV200.A45   1999   99-38520
796.52'2--dc21   CIP

Cover design by Richard Ferguson
Text design by Sheryl Mehary

BookPartners, Inc.
P. O. Box 922
Wilsonville, Oregon 97071

To David
and our sons,
Zachary Cosmo
and
Andrew Forest

Contents

Acknowledgments

Thank you to Ursula and Thorn Bacon of BookPartners; to Jane McGary, my editor; and to Susan York and Jim Acee for their valuable comments.

Prologue

We made it—exhausted and cold, but exhilarated. All of a sudden, everything that I had been working for had been accomplished: I stood at the top of the highest mountain in the world. At that moment, I realized that in the end, every summit boils down to what you're willing to risk to pursue your passion and make your dreams come true.

There is always risk. Even on relatively easy terrain, when conditions seem perfect, the sense of danger is very real when the wind kicks up and the clouds descend. But for most people who climb, the danger is not what draws them to the mountains; rather, it is the possibility of controlling risk. Climbers are drawn by the potential to test our skills, knowledge, and judgment—the opportunity to push ourselves beyond our limits.

Climbing is about the unexpected. It doesn't matter how many times a mountain or rock face has been climbed: for each person it's a new experience, and one in which the outcome is never guaranteed. Climbing is about curiosity. What's around the next hill, around the next bend? Can it be done? Can I do it? Climbing is about human relationships: developing bonds of trust and respect that demand honesty and strength—that inevitably bind you together with your partners through essential experiences of life and death.

In my life I have been privileged to be a part of the elite climbing world, where I observed myself and others in situations that test human endurance, resilience, and creativity in the most literal way. I hope that my reflections on those experiences will help you climb your own mountains and offer you a springboard for further reflections of your own.

1

A Leap of Faith

It became clear to me on a hot, dry, breezy afternoon. I was standing at the base of Smith Rock, a 500-foot mass of volcanic tuff that rises from the flatlands of central Oregon. Smith Rock and its outcroppings are the climbing capital of Oregon and draw climbers from around the world.

I'd spent that day bouldering—doing short technical climbing exercises—with Curt Haire, Evelyn Lees, and Chris Mannix. We'd worked up a good sweat in the heat, and I turned my face up, letting the rising breeze cool my neck.

That's when I saw her poised on the skyline, silhouetted by the blazing sun. She must have been 450 feet up then, most of the way to the top of the rock. Seeing her there, climbing in the distance, sent a shiver down my back.

"Who is that?" I asked.

Curt took out his binoculars and followed my gaze. "It's Shari Kearney."

"She's a great climber!"

And at that moment, that was everything I wanted to be.

I wanted to climb, and not always in the shadow of a better climber. It's easy to let your partner pull you up. If you're with someone who knows what he or she is doing, it's very easy to let that person lead all day—to sit back safely while the more experienced climber makes all the decisions and takes most of the chances. But I wasn't about to spend the rest of my life following. I had a restless itch in the deep core of my spine. I was ready to push for freedom, for the liberation that would come when I could climb either side of the rope. Eventually, I had to try for myself.

Curt put away his binoculars and nodded to Chris. "You have any preferences?" They looked over the rock, examining the features of its various faces.

I looked at my toes and kicked at the dust. "I'd like to try a lead."

Curt and Chris looked at each other for a moment. "Are you sure?" Chris asked, hands on his hips. "It's not as easy as it looks. You might want to get a little more experience first."

I shrugged. "Now's as good a time as any, don't you think?"

Curt looked at Chris, who said, "Why not?"

Evelyn smiled. "Well, yeah," she said, "it is about time we learned how to lead ourselves."

After a few minutes we decided to start on Bookworm, a sixty-foot crack etching a shadow straight up the face of a broken-off slab that leans against the central tower of Smith Rock. As I walked to the base of the climb, my heart surged. While I roped up, Curt put a hand on my shoulder.

"Are you ready?"

"Yeah." I yanked on the rope to test the knot and looked up. "I'm ready."

In climber's parlance, the front end of the rope is the smart end. The leader picks the route, locates the best holds, and places the protection that will stop a falling climber from hurtling into the void. Decisions made by the lead climber have an immediate impact not only on her life, but also on the life of the trailing climber.

Approaching the rock, I started up, slowly lingering over my first holds, carefully choosing the next ones, setting a new hexagonal aluminum chock into the crack every five feet to anchor the rope. Gaining altitude gave me confidence, though, and I developed a comfortable rhythm.

The gap was thin at first, a relatively easy jamcrack with plenty of nooks into which I could wedge my hands, and crannies to torque my feet into stable holds. But my momentum wavered when the crack widened, yawning into a more difficult off-width gap, the wrong size for fist or forearm. I had to wedge almost an entire arm inside in order to brace myself, and that disturbed my balance. My movements slowed and grew awkward. My mouth got parched, and my palms slick with sweat.

"How do you feel?" Curt called up from his position below me.

"Okay!"

I wiped the sweat from my brow. Curt's voice echoed against the face of the rock. "You're doing great!"

I looked up at my next hold. So far, so good. But for how long?

The next five feet didn't pose much of a problem. The crack was wider than below, but still snug enough to hold the largest hexagonal chock I was carrying. But as it widened even more, I found that I had only one piece large enough to fit securely into the gap.

I clung to the rock, feeling my left calf turn rubbery with strain. I knew I'd have to change my strategy. Rather than setting new protection every six feet, as I'd been able to do in the narrower gap, I'd have to set my one large chock, move up a few feet, then reach down, pull it out, and reset it above me. It would be an exhausting and frightening routine: I would suddenly be making complex moves with my closest piece of protection twelve feet below me.

On the bottom end of the rope, with someone belaying you from above, risk is always limited. In that position, you might fall all of a foot or two before your partner caught you. But now, as the leader, I could count only on the protection I'd placed myself. I could fall ten or fifteen feet before the rope caught me. And even then, there was the chance that the pieces I'd set would pop out of the crack and send me spiraling all the way down to the ground.

A thin, cool haze of panic started to drift over me. Even standing securely, I imagined myself slipping. Fear was all over my body: a hard knot in my stomach, a metallic taste on my tongue, the wings of failure fluttering against my knees.

I was so close. The lip of the slab, glinting against the empty, light blue sky, was only sixteen feet above me. I swallowed hard and crept upward, jamming an arm in the crack to hold my weight, wrenching my knee into the crack, then jamming my other arm and repeating the series of movements.

I felt my breath hot against the rock, my heart squeezed tight by adrenaline. I was exhausted from the strain, hands slick with fear, fists seeming to slip, the weight of my body drawn into the void. Spinning with a sudden wave of vertigo, I jammed my knee deep into the crack, wedging it hard against the cool interior of the rock.

Curt's voice echoed up: "Are you okay?"

Now the top of the slab was only six feet away. I had to move again or risk depleting my muscles. I reached up to jam my arm higher in the crack, but now my knee was jammed so securely I couldn't budge it. I strained to free myself, but only gently—the sharp edge of the rock was digging into my flesh. If I pulled too hard, I might lose my balance and topple. With my protection already three feet below me, that would mean falling at least six feet, then bouncing against the hard face.

"How are you doing?" Curt shouted again.

"I can't move!" The sweat on my neck had turned icy. I started to tremble.

Then everything exploded. Strangled by vertigo, I stayed glued to the rock, too frightened to move. My frazzled nerves and deepening muscle fatigue set my knees trembling, and soon I was experiencing "sewing-machine legs," the wild vibration that marks the final descent into full-blown panic. I was frozen on the rock, too terrified to look up or down. The edge of my vision blurred, and I stared straight ahead, as if hypnotized by the shadows of the crack.

Chris saw my predicament from the ground. He threw on his backpack, rushed to the easy side of the slab, and started clambering up.

"Just hold on!" I could hear Curt below me, though I didn't dare look down to him. "We'll get you down, just hold on up there!" I tightened my grip and focused on the rock two inches in front of my nose. Somewhere nearby I could hear Chris scrambling up the face, grunting with effort, the contents in his pack jangling as he moved. Then I heard him above me.

"Hey down there."

I glanced up cautiously. He was doing something with a rope, tying it to something, then clipping a locking carabiner—a metal ring that opens and closes with a screw mechanism—to a knot on the bottom. "I want you to grab onto this line," he said, "and then clip the carabiner onto your harness. Think you can do that?"

"Yeah."

When the end of the rope reached me, I coaxed my right hand free and grabbed for the carabiner. After I clipped in, Chris held the line taut, belaying me so I could feel safe unhitching my knee and elbows from the grasp of the crack. Finally loose, and with the line holding me safe from above, I relaxed enough to make my way to the crest.

The paralyzing fear vanished once I managed to clip onto Chris's rope. After a few moments on top, even my embarrassment faded. By the time Curt climbed up, I was back on my feet, leaning over the edge to greet him.

"Well, you're awful chipper now," he said, "for someone who thought she was gonna be dead about five minutes ago."

Reflections

Making the move. Actually, I was ecstatic. It seems odd, but as we coiled the rope and prepared to head back down, I couldn't wait to get back on the rock and try again. I'd felt the freedom of leading. I'd learned how hard it was, and even if I hadn't pulled it off, at least I could sense the possibilities. The promise of the future was a physical pull as strong as the tang of fear had been on the rock. I could see beyond the mistakes I'd made, and I knew that as long as I kept trying, I'd only get better.

I was nineteen years old then, and I knew I would not be content always to follow. I wanted to test my new skills and go to the next level.

Many people reach a critical time when they have to make a leap of faith. Unless I tried, I'd never know what I was capable of doing. We can either sit back and wish, or get up and act.

No one has all the skills and knowledge to succeed at a complex endeavor on the first try. But we have to get moving. Preparation is essential, but we can't spend our lifetime just preparing to prepare.

Of course, you have to be smart about it. Weigh the risks, but don't let the mere fact that risk exists paralyze you. Take out your protection and move upward. The risk is worth it.

Taking the lead. It's easy to become complacent and let others take the lead all the time. To really achieve our full potential, though, we must challenge ourselves. Are you satisfied letting someone else take the lead? Or are you ready to pull out your security and take the initiative?

When a person holds back from leading out of fear of rocking the boat, even though he or she knows what must be done to move an endeavor forward, the frustration itself can be debilitating. How many people hesitate to ask for more responsibility in their jobs because they fear that their superiors will interpret it as criticism? How many good ideas never see the light of day because the capable people who conceptualize them don't believe they can convince others?

The first step to becoming a leader is recognizing the aspiration in oneself. I did that at Smith Rock. In order to bring that aspiration into the light, into existence, I had to make that leap of faith. I didn't do everything right, but it gave me a baseline against which to gauge the abilities I knew would improve as I worked.

2

Know Your Limits—and Stretch

When Bobby Knight and Chris Mannix invited me to climb Mt. Huntington with them, it was an opportunity I just couldn't pass up. Although I had little experience on steep ice routes, I expected that, if nothing else, sheer determination and will would get me to the top.

I looked up at Huntington, a dark silhouette against the vast, incandescent eastern sky of Alaska. I was determined to propel myself up into the light atop this 18,000-foot peak, and I knew it wouldn't be easy. A few days earlier, anchoring the ropes in a steep ice gully had not been easy for me; Chris and Bobby had done all the serious work, while I watched and tried to learn the principles of protecting an ice climb.

Once we'd set foot on the mountain, it didn't take long for all of us to realize how far I'd ventured from the margin of my experience. Climbing a desert bluff on a balmy, windless day was one thing; on an ice-sheathed cliff swept by stiff, gusty winds, I didn't know what I was doing. Chris and Bobby, though, tried to be patient.

Bobby and Chris climbed easily, but for me the vertical ice was slow, painstaking work. The guys were climbing ahead and switching off leads, leaving me to depend on the rope. I was hooked onto my harness with a jumar, a finger-length metal ratcheting device that attaches to a climbing rope and slides up but not down, but it was difficult for me to get the front points of my crampons to stick in the ice. Even after I reached the gentler slopes of the couloir—the glacial gully that provided our route—each step was tiresome and painful. Kicking in the crampons and whacking with my ice ax, I took a full day to climb 750 feet. As the hours of effort passed, my arms ached and my calves burned from the constant front pointing—standing on my tiptoes with the front spikes of my crampons stuck in the ice.

Being scared didn't help matters either. Drained by anxiety and consumed by frustration, I trailed Chris and Bobby by as much distance as our rope would allow, working as hard as I could just to keep from slowing them down. When we finally climbed out of the couloir at the end of the first day, I nearly collapsed where they sat resting on a small ice shelf. By the time I sat down, they were standing up again, ready to go.

"We'll go up and set some lines for tomorrow," Chris said. "Why don't you clear away some space for our tent while we're gone?"

With the daylight still strong at the end of the subarctic afternoon, I swung my ice ax to smooth the ice beneath our tent. Temporarily relieved of the pain of climbing, I felt a wave of guilt wash over me. I hadn't led a segment of the climb all day, and even as a follower I hadn't come close to keeping up.

As I lay in the tent that night, huddled deep into my sleeping bag and still shivering in the high-altitude cold, I couldn't escape the obvious conclusion: if I weren't slowing them down, Bobby and Chris would be in a much better position to make the summit tomorrow. My dream of dashing up the mountain as easily as I had scampered up rock cliffs in Arizona was just that: a fantasy of the misinformed.

The next day was just as hard. I didn't quite trust my ice tools to hold me, and the thought of falling kept me rigid with terror. I crawled upward, the muscles in my calves knotting with the pressure. After almost losing my footing twice in the space of three steps, I felt tears starting to burn down my cheeks. I was so useless. What was I doing here? By the time I reached Chris and the end of the first rope, I was choked with frustration, tears dripping down my chin. He looked at me as I approached and a smile flickered across his face.

"So, do you want to lead the next pitch?"

My shoulders heaved with sobs. "I can't!" I finally shouted. I wiped cold tears from my chin and looked down at my crampons, glinting against the ice. "I'm scared!"

Chris gave me a hug, but I knew what he was thinking. I couldn't keep up. I'd come to Huntington unprepared, and now he and Bobby had to take up the slack.

After a few minutes, Bobby caught up to us. As he reached the top of the rope, he bent over, gasping in the thin, cold air. When he stood up straight again, I noticed how pale his face was.

"Bobby, are you okay?"

After pausing for a drink of water, Bobby shrugged. "Got a headache," he said. "Dizzy. Been feeling kind of puky, too."

We all knew the symptoms of altitude sickness: headaches, nausea, dizziness, loss of appetite. Bobby wasn't desperately ill, but it obviously wasn't a good idea for him to go much higher. Still, we were so close to the summit! And after coming this far, Bobby wasn't about to surrender our chance for making the top. He took another drink and then volunteered to lead the next pitch.

The summit was in our sights, about 200 vertical feet away— perhaps a three-hour climb, given the cross-slope traversing we'd have to do. And if Bobby wasn't going to stop, I sure wasn't going to add to my disgrace by sitting around waiting for them to get down. As long as they kept going, I had to move with them.

Bobby took the lead, and after a few deep breaths, he started up again. He went only a hundred feet before he hit the rock. The tip of his ice ax glanced through the ice and slammed into the underlying rock full force. The impact broke the metal tip free from the shaft. As he stood there numbly holding the empty fiberglass handle, Bobby knew our climb had just ended.

Sitting in our tent that night, back on the glacier, I apologized for being so slow. "You could have done so much better," I said. "I ruined it for you."

"Aw, you didn't ruin it for us," Chris said.

"But I didn't know what I was doing," I protested.

"Forget it," Bobby interjected. "We climbed the couloir, and that's what we came here for. After that, the summit hardly matters. It was just a walk. A formality. Like picking up a diploma. What's more important: going to school or going to graduation?"

I shrugged.

"You got an education," Chris said.

I did indeed.

Reflections

Knowing our limits. Have you ever felt completely overwhelmed when you've gotten yourself into something way over your head? But then you may have thought, "No, this is good for me. I'm stretching myself. I'm getting out of my comfort zone."

There is a fine line between challenging ourselves and overstepping our limits. I had built a lot of self-confidence along the way to Mt. Huntington, but I didn't realize my limits. I'd leaped forward to a much more difficult climb than I had accomplished up to that time, without taking the time to learn and hone my skills. I was unprepared for this mountain. The higher we climbed, the more my frustration grew and my self-confidence dropped.

So often we take on projects that look interesting, capture our imagination, and challenge us, only to find out that what we had thought was a mere stretch is really a monster. And we fall flat on our faces. We become overwhelmed and frustrated; we fall behind on the project; we may procrastinate and eventually become altogether immobilized.

After my first big ice climb, I vowed this would never happen to me again. I certainly had the desire to climb and the passion to climb, but this was not enough. I had to develop the ability and experience. I had to become competent. It would take courage to commit myself to the gradual learning of these challenging skills.

I am a firm believer in pushing oneself against limits. However, the first stage in moving beyond our limits is knowing what those are. This requires taking a good hard honest look at our abilities—both strengths and weaknesses. We must know where we are before we can decide where we want to be.

Building competence gradually. The second stage is taking realistically small steps. Mastery is not achieved in one day. Start with where you are now and progress slowly. Practice your new skills on a regular basis and build a strong foundation. When you have built your skills, you will feel a sense of self-confidence, and with it, stability and comfort.

Every new skill and every increase in knowledge empowers us. Educating ourselves is a process of building up the power we will need to accomplish our goals.

It's important to choose your challenges with your competence in mind. If a climb is too easy, climbers get bored; they're not motivated, and they don't feel much satisfaction when they reach the summit. As the level of challenge and risk rises, so does the level of pride and satisfaction in meeting them. However, when the climb is too difficult and the chance of success is low, the people attempting it may become scared, stressed, anxious, and frustrated. Build on small successes; don't set yourself up to be proved inadequate. Be realistic in your learning: find what challenges you and stretches you, but not something impossible for you today.

Examining experiences. Whether we succeed or fail at it, the most challenging climb in the world will not help us grow unless we take the time for reflection. Unexamined experiences don't produce insights. Insights and wisdom come with reflection and analysis. Learn from your experiences. What did you do well? What needs to improve? What can you accept from your mentors and apply in your next challenge?

Preparing to contribute. One person can bring the entire team down through failure to prepare. It wasn't just frustration that made this experience so unpleasant. I also felt guilty about not pulling the same weight as my partners. Instead of helping propel us upward, I was dragging us down. Chris and Bobby had to work overtime to compensate for my inability to lead.

When we don't have the skills and knowledge needed for the task at hand, someone else will have to take up the slack. How do you feel when you take up the slack for coworkers who can't contribute their fair share? Or are you the person who's not taking full responsibility? If you're experiencing imbalances like this at work, could they be corrected if the less competent team members improved their skills?

Learning from others. If you're working hard at building skills, develop a support system. You can do it alone, but it's a lot more difficult. Having the support of other people to share the challenges, joys, and risks makes the work seem easier. The psychological support from other people helps us build our confidence and makes learning more fun. Find a person or two who will act as your mentors, or join a group that includes experienced, sympathetic members.

My partners were patient and supportive, and I was able to come away from the experience without bitterness and with renewed resolve to improve. If you're in the position of dealing with a partner or coworker who is in over his head, try to resolve the situation in a supportive way. Everyone involved will be better for the experience.

Know others' limits. At this time in my career, I wasn't ready to lead the climbing party. My partners were kind enough to offer me the opportunity, but they didn't push me into a role I couldn't sustain. The worst thing an employer can do is to throw people into jobs they don't have the skill, knowledge, and experience to handle. Hiring is a risk: match the risk to the level of competence.

With two young children, I'm starting to notice the way this principle applies in my family life too. Expecting too much of children too early puts tremendous pressure on them and creates stress in their lives and by extension the lives of their parents.

We're pushing them to know more at a younger age than we ever did, and developmentally they may not be ready for it.

Accepting individual responsibility. In the final analysis, building competence is each person's individual responsibility. We've all heard the expression "Ignorance is bliss." Ignorance is ignorance. It is not bliss on a mountain and it is not bliss in business or at home. What you don't know will hurt you.

We saw a perfect example of this as the 1996 Mt. Everest tragedy unfolded. Wealthy people had paid experienced guides to take them up the mountain. They paid someone else for the knowledge, skills, and experience they hadn't taken the time to acquire on their own. The chance of dying above 26,000 feet on Everest is 30 percent, whether one is experienced or not. When you hand your life over to someone else on a mountain—when you haven't taken the time to learn the skills and gain experience, knowledge, and judgment—you have no power to take care of yourself.

How much do you know about the skills and processes that are important in your own life and work? Is it enough to make the decisions that affect your success, and to guarantee the economic survival of you and your associates?

3

Will to Live

Mt. Robson is an isolated 13,000-foot peak in the Canadian Rockies of Alberta. In fall of 1980, my partner Curt Haire and I made the two-day hike to Robson Lake, then set out for the glacier beneath the mountain. We traveled light in the summery weather, planning to set up our tent and catch a few hours of sleep before starting up the mountain early the next morning. Assuming things went well the next day, we'd make the summit by early afternoon, then retreat down the easier east slope and be back to our tent on the glacier by nightfall.

But the icy north face of the mountain was more difficult to climb than we'd imagined, and it took us more than ten hours to find our way to the summit. By then the sun had started its long slide to the western horizon, and we both knew we wouldn't have enough light to find our way down. Still, a night on the summit didn't seem too awful a fate. With clear skies we'd see a spectacular sunset, then bivouac under the stars. And with the can of tuna, crackers, and candy bars stashed in our packs, we'd even have a halfway decent dinner.

We ate quickly, exhausted from our climb. Then we put on our anoraks, pulled our hats down over our ears, and huddled together in a shallow snow pit. As the fireball sun sank into a blood-red horizon, I nestled my head against Curt's chest. My thoughts drifted off into the sky, and I was asleep before the last light faded.

When my eyes fluttered open a few hours before dawn, Curt was already awake. I could feel his arm tight around my shoulders. I could tell something was wrong.

The clouds had descended after we'd fallen asleep. Soon snow started falling, and by dawn we were sitting in a full-on blizzard. At first I was almost too shocked to believe it. How did this happen? We had always been so conscious of the weather, always ready for anything to happen!

Being prepared is perhaps the most important credo for a climber. And we both knew it. You can't take anything for granted in the mountains, no matter how mild and lovely the environment may seem when you set out. But this one time we took a risk, and now, caught in the bowels of a white-out storm, we had to pay the price.

Our situation seemed bleak. We had no food or water. We didn't have a tent or sleeping bags. The north face was far too steep for us to risk descending in the driving wind and snow. The heavy clouds showed no sign of clearing, and we couldn't see anything beyond the tips of our own mittens. The temperature continued to drop.

"This is serious trouble," Curt said. For the moment, we had no idea if we'd ever be able to find a route out of danger. But it's a reality of mountaineering that when crisis hits, you can't allow emotions to interrupt logical thought. As soon as it was light, we began to scrape our way through the blizzard, searching for a way down the mountain.

We got one break—in the dull light after dawn, we found a faint set of day-old footprints leading down the eastern face. We weren't certain where the steps led, but they were our only hope, our only clue to the way off the mountain. We followed them for the next ten hours, hunkered together against the unyielding winds and hard stinging snow. When we lost the path, we'd criss-cross the slope, bent almost double to search for the slight dimples in the thickening white blanket. But we always managed to find them again somehow, and in the gathering murk of dusk we found ourselves at what we thought was the top of the Kain Face, a 45-degree ice face that stands as the main obstacle on Robson's east side.

As night closed in, we got ready to feel our way down the ice face. The snow and wind had lessened in the darkness, but still the clouds swirled around us. As Curt twisted in the first ice screw, I sat on the snow, my arms wrapped tightly against my chest. Hoping to find a hint of a landmark, I strained my eyes for focus and tried to bore through the impenetrable silver blanket. Shivering and aching with exhaustion, I tried desperately to pierce the fog, but as night slipped up on us, nothing swirled into focus.

We continued in the dark, wearing headlamps to illuminate our movements. The slim beams of light disappeared into nothingness, but we had to keep going. We had to get off the exposed ridge, down to where we could bivouac for a few hours without facing the killing wind.

I down-climbed beneath Curt, moving slowly, kicking for footholds, mustering my energy every time I swung my ice ax. Every thirty-five feet I'd set an ice screw into the ice, using the pick of my ice ax to twist it in, then stringing our rope through the carabiner. When the wind gusted, I'd squeeze in toward the slope, feeling the cold, bony fingers brush against my sides. The night magnified the tug of gravity. Every step pulled at the tendons wiring my legs and rattled the ladder of vertebrae in my spine. My eyes dimmed; my brain waves seemed to flatten. I hadn't eaten for twenty-four hours. I hadn't had a drink for more than twelve hours. I'd barely stopped moving since dawn. I wondered how much more I could take.

Chunks of ice careened down the slope. Every time Curt swung his ice ax, a bit of the slope would give way, skittering and sailing down on top of me. The shrapnel got larger as time passed. After an hour the ice chunks were fist-sized, falling in abrupt showers that slammed against my helmet and pounded my shoulders.

I moved onward automatically, each motion draining my energy, like a pendulum swinging in ever smaller arcs. I heard an oncoming shower of ice chunks and tried to lean out of the way, but I lost a foothold and almost fell. Gasping and clinging desperately to the ice, I tried to reassemble my wits. Shivering with cold and hunger, dazed with thirst, I stood on the slope and waited for Curt. In the darkness below, the ice face vanished into the clouds. Above me, the rope to Curt faded into the darkness. If I fell, the rope would be the only thing keeping me from the clouds below. The last thin barrier between life and death.

I watched the rope tremble with Curt's movements, and I pulled in the slack as he came closer. I contemplated its flimsy weight. In that instant another ice chunk came cracking against the side of my helmet, an explosion of white light in my head, another sharp jolt for my body.

In that moment I wondered why I was bothering at all. I was so cold and hungry and tired; I had already felt so much raw pain. It was too much. What was the point of going on? In the air ahead of me the rope jiggled again. If I took out my knife, I could cut it in an instant. Then I could jump. No more cold. No more hunger. The misery would end, and then there'd be a blissful emptiness, a world beyond blisters and hunger cramps and parched, cracked lips. It would be so easy to slip away.

This is not going to happen. The hard shell of my resolve re-formed, and I was moving again. When we got to the bottom of the ice face an hour later, we dug a trench in the snow and sat scrunched together, conserving our body heat by folding our knees up against our chests. With the wind roaring and the snow still rushing around us, I'd sink into brief, shallow sleep, only to rattle awake with my own violent shivering. The night seemed to last forever. Sometimes I tried to relax enough to stop shivering: I'd curl into myself, limp as a rag, and the vibrating would end. A strange peace for thirty seconds, perhaps a minute, then my muscles would seize up and my jaw would clatter uncontrollably.

"It'd be easy to give up. Just lie down and give in to it," I said to Curt.

"A lot of people do," he said. "We'll keep going. Once morning comes." And we sat together, shivering and breathing, waiting for the dawn to come.

And it would come, and we would live to see it. I'd made the decision up on the ice face, when the ice was raining down and the rope dangled so thin and delicate. The moment I snapped awake up there, the resolve was even harder and more deeply rooted than it had been before. In the face of everything, I knew I would keep moving. I knew that hunger would pass, that pain would end, and that at some point I'd be able to close my eyes. I willed myself to survive, to keep going, step after painful step, until we got back.

When it did get light and we saw how the clouds had lifted from the mountain, we could see the glacier only a hundred feet beneath us, and right then, I saw everything else too. Food, warmth, rest. I saw my life. We were back at our tent by one p.m.

Reflections

The extreme choice. Years later I'd realize how often people make another choice—how a struggle to survive leads to a crossroads. The extreme choice, the one I made on Mt. Robson, is between life and death. I stood there for a moment and made a conscious decision. You either sit down and die, or you keep moving.

When people consciously decide to give up, their dreams may die, leaving them bereft and despairing. Some people choose to give up when they are confronted with obstacles that at the time seem to be overwhelming. They resign themselves to lives without happiness or achievement—lives of "quiet desperation."

As long as a human being—or an animal, for that matter—is physically capable of continuing to live, that being has an amazing capacity for continued striving. When you think you can't cope with pain or adversity, it helps to remember: I'm not alone; this is something that many people face. It's not too big for me. Having chosen not to die establishes a bedrock in the mind; it will make you depend on yourself in the future as few other acts can do. Each time we make the decision to keep moving, it strengthens our foundation.

Learning to endure. Many people today, especially in wealthy Western nations, are unprepared for uncomfortable or difficult situations. The service economy thrives by making everything easier, and with every generation people are swathed more closely in layers of protection against both the natural environment and disease or injury. There are fewer and fewer opportunities to learn the crucial lessons of endurance and discipline.

How many of us give up when things merely get uncomfortable? While it's true that we won't die if we drop out of school, end a relationship, or abandon a job, we are still compromising our drive to succeed. Every time we succumb to the temptation of resignation, we are weakening our innate natural instinct to survive. When we finally face a truly life-threatening challenge, that instinct may not be strong enough to preserve us.

Focusing on essentials. I've been asked how I deal with the inevitable pain of a grueling climb. I do it by compartmentalizing: separating my feeling of discomfort and what I think about it from what I have to keep focused on. A person can recognize pain and difficulty, but still set it aside in the mind. If my feet are literally freezing, I have to deal with it so I won't lose them to frostbite; but if they're just cold, I don't have to foreground that fact. That information won't help propel me to my goal: it will just drag me down.

It's counterproductive to divert attention to a problem we can't correct while we need to do something else. If we are in a truly serious situation, we can't lose our focus even when we experience something terrible. When I led an expedition to K2, one of the climbers, Dan Culver, died in a fall above 26,000 feet. Despite our grief, we could not allow our emotions to take over. We still had to spend one more night at that altitude. The next day, we found ourselves in a whiteout, with the wind gusting over 100 miles per hour. We had to focus absolutely just to get the rest of the team off the mountain alive.

Sometimes, instead of compartmentalizing obstructions, people perceive them as reasons to give up. In nonindustrial nations we see many people who are obviously doing hard work every day despite physical problems that most of us would consider disabling.

Our own grandparents probably did the same thing. Do you notice a lack of productivity in your endeavor as a result of too much focus on problems that could be set aside?

4

Daring to Dream

When Curt and I finally got to Alaska in mid-May, we loaded ourselves and our gear into a Cessna and took off for the McKinley staging area on the Kahiltna Glacier. Flying in, I searched the wild terrain until the mountain finally came into view, soaring up from among the cottonball clouds hovering around its shoulder. I felt my mouth open; an involuntary gasp swelled my chest. As much as I'd read about McKinley, as much as I'd memorized the routes and studied photographs to learn the contours of its ridges, I was still stunned by how breathtakingly big it was. Not only tall—over 20,000 feet—but wide. And steep. Even in Alaska's great empty expanse of wilderness and tundra, this one mountain seemed to dominate the sky. The sight made my heart dance.

In the last four years I'd worked my way up a lot of mountains—more than a dozen peaks in the Cascades and the Sierras. I'd made mistakes and had breakthroughs; I'd taken the steps one after another. Eventually I'd turned myself into a serious mountaineer. And at this point it was the one thing I knew I could do: the one set of achievements I could point to as the defining

moments in my adult life. And if that was true—if climbing was
what I chose to do—I was determined to become a great climber.
I'd stood up to a lot of challenges, and now vast McKinley and its
jagged Cassin Ridge felt like the obvious place to put everything I
knew to the test. If I could climb the sharp ice ridge, I'd come away
knowing that I could go beyond North America.

Just after dawn, we sank our spikes into the 1,500-foot
Japanese Couloir on the Cassin Ridge. The climbing came slow and
difficult on the sheer blue ice, and it took nine hours to reach the
Cassin Ledge, a four-by-fifteen-foot rock ledge that marks the top
of the couloir. We spent two nights camped on the shelf, taking the
extra day in our tent to adjust to the altitude. Then we headed up
into the rocky part of the ridge.

Climbing in the arctic wind with a sixty-pound backpack
strapped to my shoulders added an entirely new challenge to the
morning. The pack not only threw off my sense of balance but
also caught the wind. The occasional wild gust would shove me
sideways, and only a well-placed handhold or two saved me
from taking a screamer back down toward the Cassin Ledge.
The top of the cliffs didn't offer much safer terrain. Once we
scaled the rock pitch we had to traverse Fantasy Ridge, a foot-
wide, snow-capped tightrope with heart-squeezing 2,000-foot
drops on either side.

After we crossed the ridge and arrived on a steep glacier, we
dug out a small ice shelf and set up our tent for the night. The
weather turned by the time we finished eating dinner. Clouds
moved in quickly, riding hard gusts of frigid wind. Snow started
falling just as the night sank around us. We went to sleep listening
to the sides of our tent tremble in the wind, and hoping the morning
would bring clearer skies and gentler breezes. But the snow only
came harder. We spent the next two days entombed in the glacier,
waiting for the storm to blow past the mountain.

Once the weather calmed enough for us to venture outside
again, we spent two more days working our way up the steep ice
and rock faces on the ridge. Then another storm blew in, and we
hunkered down on a thin ice mantle just above 18,000 feet,
tentbound for two more days.

Even with the fits of violent weather, the climb was going well. Curt and I had already spent a week at high altitude, and so far neither of us had developed any physical problems. Huddled in my sleeping bag, I could sense the lifelessness around me. A sharp surge of adrenaline shot needles through my body as I realized we were finally out on the edge. Closing my eyes in the dark, I could envision us against the night, small specks of warmth adrift in the frozen wilderness. Being that alone, that exposed to the forces of a vast, indifferent world, was both terrifying and thrilling. If we were going to survive up here, it was because we were strong enough and smart enough to keep ourselves alive.

As Curt and I toiled on the icy upper reaches of the Cassin, I knew we were gaining momentum. The crest of the ridge was in front of us. A hundred yards away, then seventy-five, then fifty. When I could count the steps, I felt a surge of emotion. Gratitude for being alive, elation from scaling the ridge—it all rushed inside me, and as I stood there, drinking in the cold, empty air above the continent, I felt free. I folded my legs and sat down. Curt knelt next to me and put his arms around my shoulders. And we sat there together for a while, looking down at the world stretching away beneath us.

As I sat there, after successfully completing one of the hardest routes on the highest mountain in North America, I abruptly realized that I wanted more. I began to fantasize. If I could climb Mt. McKinley, then why not Everest, the highest mountain in the world? I was so startled by my thought I quickly looked over at Curt, just to make sure he couldn't read my mind. Suddenly I felt embarrassed and discouraged. Who was I to think I could climb Everest?

Reflections

Have you ever caught yourself doing that? Looking around to make sure no one was reading your thoughts? What if someone discovered your wildest dream? What would Curt think of me if he knew I wanted to climb Everest? Would he laugh? Would he ridicule me?

Have you ever dismissed yourself or abandoned your dreams because you were afraid of what others might think of you? Sometimes our fear of what we think others might think of us can cause us to give up our aspirations. Long before anyone else has the chance to dismiss us, we do it to ourselves.

Curt wasn't the one judging me; he didn't even know what I was thinking. I was the one judging me. Our fear of what others may think of us is an expression of our own insecurities. Those insecurities will shrink only when we start thinking positively.

If we think only negative thoughts, we will get only negative outcomes. Negative thinking can be a downward spiral that saps more and more of a person's energy. It can leave us frozen in inactivity.

To take control, we have to start by paying attention to the conversations going on in our heads. Don't think automatic thoughts; think purposeful thoughts. Make the conversations in your head something that will lift you up, not tear you down. Tell yourself that I can, not I can't.

How many of your dreams are limited by the beliefs you hold in your mind about yourself? Dealing with self-doubt has to be a conscious process. Look honestly at both your strengths and weaknesses to identify what is valid in your doubts and what is not. If you're not sure, ask a trusted friend. When you've identified the actual weaknesses, what actions can you take to rectify them?

5

Learn, Commit, Act

I rapped—tentatively—on the door and tried to hide my butterflies with a smile. Inside, I heard footsteps coming closer. We shook hands and Sue Giller ushered me in. "We wanted to give a young climber a chance to go to the Himalayas. To gain some experience. And you were on the Cassin Ridge? A tough route. Ama Dablam shouldn't be much of a leap for you."

I was relieved by the way Sue put me at ease and offered her praise in welcoming me. I was also humbled and honored to be going to the Himalayas with a group of experienced, competent women.

I was very impressed with Sue's super-organized leadership. Schooled by her father, a career army officer, Sue had plotted out the expedition like a general sending the troops into Normandy. The expedition's finances and equipment procurement schedules were measured on charts. One set of graphs tracked each climber's work days and rest days on the mountain. Another set showed the progress of the team as a whole—the equipment being hauled and the food and supplies needed along the way.

As a latecomer to the expedition, I didn't have many pre-climb responsibilities. I volunteered to track down a few dozen pairs of polypropylene long underwear, however, and to work on a little fund-raising for last-minute expenses. Most of the executives I spoke to were happy to donate a few dollars to something as novel as an all-woman expedition. Only one fellow didn't seem to understand the spirit of the climb. He was interested in donating, though, and we had quite a few conversations before he called to finalize the offer.

"Just one last thing," he said. There was silence, and then he cleared his throat. "You gals will pose for pictures on the mountain with our logo, right?"

"That's part of the deal," I said. "And if everything goes right we'll even do it on the summit."

"Oh, good," he said. "That's excellent. Exactly what we were hoping." A pause, then another "ahem." "But, what do you usually wear when you take the pictures?"

"What do we wear?"

"I mean, you pose in bikinis, right?"

We decided we could probably get by without the benefit of that particular donation.

The expedition left the United States at the beginning of March, flying from Chicago to Germany, then to Delhi and finally to Kathmandu, Nepal. Just stepping out of the airplane and onto the tarmac, I could feel the Third World brushing against me. The sun was strong and the heavy air thick with a sweet, pungent smell: rotting vegetables, the remnants of the wandering sacred cows, the sour odor of poverty. On the steps of the airport we found lines of beggars, crippled and maimed, legless men pushing themselves on plywood boards equipped with rusty wheels.

The suffering was hard to watch, but away from the airport the city was alive and exciting. The streets were narrow but jammed with people, the men in grimy T-shirts and shorts, the women in colorful cotton saris. The entire city seemed to be late for an appointment, everyone tearing around on bicycles, bells chiming and wheels clanking on the pavement.

We spent a day or two resting in Kathmandu, then rode a creaky bus up into the hills, out to where the road ended. From there we launched a hundred-mile trek on winding mountain paths. Springtime was beautiful in the hills of Nepal. The mornings were cold and crisp, the sky a deep royal blue, and the rolling hills velvety with green vegetation. The days would warm as the sun rose, and with our small army of porters in tow, we'd troop up dusty paths and across thin footbridges. Up past the terraced farms that carved the hills into green stairsteps, across the silver streams knifing down the valleys, beneath thirty-foot rhododendron bushes bursting with bright pink blossoms.

The ground turned rockier and the terrain less luxurious as we gained altitude. After sixteen days we reached our base camp, just beneath the base of the mountain on a desolate plateau at 16,500 feet. We set up our tents on rocky, subalpine land, next to a small, glacier-fed pond. The terrain was gaunt and brown in the early spring, but still nourishing enough to support the local yak population. The huge, furry creatures were regular visitors to our camp, pausing to drink from the pond or nibble at the sparse grasses sprouting from between the rocks.

I already knew the reputations of most of the women on the expedition, but I got to know them as people during our trek and while we set up base camp. All of them were experienced climbers. Shari Kearney was in her late twenties by then and had climbed her share of big mountains, as had her new housemate from Montana, a lanky six-footer named Lucy Smith. Both Shari and Lucy were instructors for the National Outdoor Leadership School, based in Lander, Wyoming. Ann MacQuarie, a twenty-five-year-old ranger at Yosemite, was just as strong and experienced and had a permit for Everest the following year. Jini Griffith, a thirty-year-old builder from Ketchum, Idaho, was a generous though very independent climber. Susan Havens, a thirtyish physical therapist from Alaska, was quiet and graceful. Our doctor came from Switzerland: Heidi Ludi was the only non-American in the group and at thirty-six was also the senior member of the expedition. Sue Giller, our leader, had climbed all around the world; Sue, Shari, Lucy, and Heidi all had previous Himalayan climbing experience.

Seen from its base, the top of Ama Dablam appears almost vertical. The peak, a face of snow and ice-covered rock, is jagged, a razor of ice scraping high against the firmament. The mountain has a distinct presence. The routes are steep and very technical, and at this time they were rarely climbed. We were only the third modern expedition to climb on Ama Dablam—the Nepalese government had kept it closed until 1980.

Our planned route took us up the mountain's southwest ridge. Most of the climb followed the ridge itself, a thin knifeblade of rock rising from the snowy face of the mountain. Snaking between climbable pitches on both sides of the ridge, you have to cross over the ridgetop several times. Along the way there is some extreme rock climbing, technical ice climbing, and then, on summit day, a long 45-degree snow slope to the summit at 22,495 feet.

The complex climb was made even more challenging by the pressure of altitude and the burden of the thin air. In Kathmandu we encountered more than one local expert who would only shake a head at our plans. So technical up there, are you sure you women can do it all by yourselves? Well, why not?

Back when Sue started climbing, just the concept of an all-woman expedition in the Himalayas would have been unthinkable. In the early 1970s, the majority of male climbers were up front about their sexism. Women, they said, just didn't have the muscle power to take on the big mountains. Also, the mountains were a sanctuary of male bonding, not to be interfered with by women. That attitude had dominated mountaineering since the sport's beginnings.

When Arlene Blum, a climber from Berkeley, decided to lead an all-woman expedition to Annapurna in 1978, the American Alpine Club hemmed and hawed about making the recommendation that the Nepalese government required for admission, even after Nepal's climbing ministry said they'd be delighted to host the group. Blum's expedition had been successful, though, despite two deaths.

An all-woman climb on Dhaulagiri the next year was less successful and lost one climber. Sue had been a member of the Dhaulagiri team, and although she had enjoyed the climb, she had not thought of leading her own all-woman team to the Himalayas until a climber named Annie Whitehouse called and offered her a permit for Ama Dablam in 1982. Sue agreed to take over Annie's permit, then started pondering climbers. She knew mixed climbs usually worked better, since the varied physical abilities and character traits of men and women can make a more complete team. But an all-woman team had its benefits, too. Raising money, she knew, would be much easier for an all-woman expedition. And with so few American women ever having climbed in the Himalayas, it was always good to give as many women as possible a chance to climb there. Each woman who did could be a role model for women climbers who had only dreamed of going.

The sexual politics of the climb held little interest for me, but once we got on the mountain, it was fun to be in a group of women. Sometimes, when men are on the team, it's easy to defer to their strength. If the going gets really tough, a woman knows she can hang back and let the more muscular men take the lead. A group of women doesn't have this luxury, which is both sobering and freeing. We had to do everything for ourselves.

And we did it quite smoothly. With Sue's careful planning, our weeks of mountainside preparation and route-setting went off like clockwork. We carried the loads up the mountain on schedule and worked and rested according to our preset agendas. Throughout, Sue was a model expedition leader. Although in peak climbing shape and itching to work on the mountain herself, she spent most of her time in base camp, sitting in a lawn chair with her charts and a bowl of popcorn, peering up at our progress through powerful binoculars. She oversaw each step from a distance, allowing all her climbers to take turns leading the way up the mountain.

When we finished setting the route, stocking our camps, and anchoring the rope up the steep flanks of the mountain, we split into two summit teams and prepared to make our move for the top.

Setting out from base camp on the first summit team with Shari and Lucy and Susan Havens, I pressed up the ridge toward the summit, feeling strong and confident. I was sure of myself on the ice. I had no problem on the steep rock pitches. I was even relaxed most of the time—in itself an improvement over the tense week and a half I'd spent inching up Mount McKinley. I was finally comfortable at altitude, understanding that I could survive in the thin air. There had been only one moment of doubt when we were setting the route. On the first night I spent above 19,000 feet, I woke up in the middle of the night wondering who'd pounded the ten-penny nails through my skull.

I was reeling. Besides the nails, there was a vise tightening around my skull, pressing the hemispheres of my brain together, squashing my fragile hypothalamus. I knew exactly what was happening. Altitude sickness. Too panicked to be polite, I sat up and screamed. Shari, huddled deep in her sleeping bag next to me, lurched up in the darkness.

"What's the matter?"

"I've got to get down," I wailed. "Right now!"

She looked up from between the folds of her bag, mumbling through a fog of sleep, "Huh?"

"I've got a headache."

"A headache?"

Now she was awake. She repeated what I said, only without any tangible concern in her voice.

"You've got a headache?"

I listed the rest of my symptoms. Or rather, the lack of other symptoms. No nausea. No gurgling. Just the headache. A terrible headache, I added. Something had to be really wrong, right?

Shari sighed. She reached into her pack for her first-aid kit. She held out her fist and dropped two aspirins into my open palm.

"Swallow these," she said. "And then go back to sleep." She dove once more beneath the surface of her sleeping bag. I woke up the next morning feeling fine.

Even as Ama Dablam's summit drew closer, one other object loomed above us: the same peak that had captured my imagination from the moment I set foot on top of the Cassin Ridge, from the moment I set foot in Nepal. No matter how much we sweated and strained to pull ourselves to the top of Ama Dablam, Mount Everest dwarfed us. She was an elusive giant on our side of the mountain, hidden behind the summit we were now trying to climb. Even when we got higher, the peak of Everest usually vanished into the cloak of clouds gathered around her shoulders. But I could still see it in my mind.

Ann and her husband, Chas, had a permit for Everest during the 1983 climbing season and were planning to bring at least three or four women. As our expedition went on, base camp conversations focused increasingly on Ann's Everest expedition. Almost everyone wanted to go, and Ann knew it. In the end she invited Shari, Lucy, and Sue.

I wanted to go, too, but I didn't dare say anything about it. I couldn't imagine asking, for one thing. I was so young, still so inexperienced. I hadn't even finished climbing my first Himalayan peak, so it seemed terribly presumptuous to imagine I could take on Everest.

But I did make it to the summit of Ama Dablam. And I stood there alongside Lucy and Shari and Susan, gazing up through the clouds, which parted momentarily to afford us one long look at the crooked rock pyramid crest that rose 6,678 feet above us.

Over a mile higher than where we stood. I was both awed and inspired. And at that moment, I made Mount Everest my true goal. I wasn't sure when I was going to climb Everest; I wasn't even sure how; I just knew that I would.

Reflections

Mentors. Sue Giller had told her team that she wanted to open an opportunity for a younger climber to gain experience in the Himalayas. One of the reasons I was invited to participate on the Ama Dablam climb was that Shari Kearney had recognized my ability. She was my mentor and exemplar.

Choosing and accepting a mentor shortens our learning curve. We don't have to rely on trial and error as we build our competence. We can ask a trusted mentor questions that we might hesitate to ask others.

One important thing we learn from a mentor is the culture of our chosen field. Climbing is a remarkably specialized culture, with its own language and an array of rules and principles that are not usually formulated in writing. Your own special field probably has comparable cultural specifics. A mentor can teach us these elements of culture in a nonthreatening, nonjudgmental way.

Who are your mentors? Can you be a mentor to someone else? It's important to give back.

Accepting your dream. Even though I had been dreaming about Everest since I stood on the peak of Mt. McKinley, my dream crystallized as I gazed at Everest from Ama Dablam. It's one thing to imagine a great goal and prepare for it; it's another to take the first irrevocable step toward it. You have to take the initiative to make your dreams come true.

When we give up on a dream, it's like being stormbound in a snow cave: afraid to move or change, frozen in an unsatisfying life by our own resignation. Live the life that you want. Follow your dreams. What fears and excuses are keeping you frozen? If you died today, what dreams would die with you?

It takes courage to set lofty goals for ourselves. It takes courage to believe in ourselves and believe we truly deserve greatness. I learned that if you're going to dream, dream big! When you dream small, you accomplish small things. When you dream big, you open up the route to accomplish great things. High achievement always takes place in the framework of high expectations.

Despite my moments of uncertainty, I went on to pursue my dream. My experiences had taught me determination and commitment. It's easy to sit at the bottom of the mountain and complain "I'm too cold," "I'm too tired," or just "I can't." But you will never realize your dreams unless you take the first steps and say "I can," "I will," and finally, "I did." Vision, belief in oneself and one's goal, and commitment give us the strength and courage to move forward.

Acting on your dream. If we sit and wait and do nothing to make our dreams come true they remain just that: a fantasy, a creation living only inside our heads. We must take action in order for our dreams to become goals to become realities. When I returned from Ama Dablam, I applied for my own Everest permit and I also began looking for another expedition to join that had already begun the permit process. When I found out that Scott Fischer, a friend whom I hadn't seen or talked to in five years, had a permit to climb Everest in 1987, I immediately called him. I awkwardly apologized for not keeping in touch, and in the same breath I asked to be considered for his team. One month, later he invited me.

Perseverance. You don't just make Mount Everest your goal and a month later go out and climb it. It takes years of preparation and planning. Back in the early 1980s, it took six to eight years to get permission to climb Everest from the Tibetan side of the mountain. If you wanted to climb Everest from the easier Nepalese side, it was an even longer wait of eight to ten years.

Waiting is not easy. Many of us have grown up in the age of immediacy and instant gratification: "If I can't get it now, forget it. If I can't get it now, then I'll move on to something else." Perseverance, or what my grandfather called "stick-to-it-iveness," is becoming a rare quality. Computers have made information available at the speed of electronic signals. Businesses adopt the motto "Just in time." Consumers want goods and services "just for me." Many young people think it takes too long to climb the corporate ladder; that's one reason we have so many new start-up businesses these days. Quick fixes and short-term thinking are rampant.

When I decided on climbing Mount Everest, I had to adjust to a much longer process of preparation than I had ever encountered before. For the next three years, I continued to climb with Everest in the back of my mind. I didn't forsake my goal, but I didn't let it consume me. The mountains I climbed did not become only a means to that end; each presented its own challenges, lessons, and rewards. I knew that when I finally had the opportunity to go to Everest, I would be that much more prepared.

When we have an overarching goal, every small opportunity may teach us something that will help us reach it eventually. We can't let our goal put blinders on us, though; we have to remember to enjoy our smaller successes too.

Now my highest goal is raising my two young children to adulthood—a time frame of decades. What is the time frame of your dream? Have you accepted its reality?

6

Ask for Help

In summer of 1986, in preparation for our Everest climb, a group of us joined some friends from Colorado on an expedition to Pik Kommunizma, a jagged mountain with razor cliffs on all sides. The tallest of the Russian Pamirs, it towers over its corner of Eurasia, cresting at just under 24,600 feet. Among the party were Scott Fischer, the Everest expedition leader; Wes Krause, the Everest co-leader and Scott's business partner; Geo Schunk, an attorney from Helena, Montana; Liz Nichol, the owner of a Colorado Springs health food store; and George Kahrl, a recent Harvard graduate.

Using a relatively lightweight approach, we planned to climb the mountain in just ten days—two weeks, if necessary.

We carried loads of equipment up to our first camp. It was a short haul to the top of the dirty glacier at just above 15,000 feet, only 1,000 feet above base camp. I was with Fredo, walking fast, the two of us pushing the front edge of the expedition. It was a short hike, but it gave us plenty of time to talk. Fredo—Steve Manfredo—was a hippie mountain man from the high reaches of

Crested Butte, Colorado. He was an experienced climber and an avid kayaker and skier.

Day one made for swift walking, and our momentum carried us into the second day for another glide up the glacial moraine. We made the traverse across the mountain, up a gradual 2,000 feet to the base of the Borodkin Ridge at 17,000 feet. Here we dumped some equipment, then scampered back down to 15,000 feet, giving ourselves a chance to acclimate to the thinner air before heading up again. We retraced our steps the next morning, across the rocky face one more time to our camp at the base of the Borodkin.

I passed Fredo on the way up and gave him the high sign as I went past. "How's it goin' today?" I asked.

He smiled and waved. "Doing okay," he said, his vowels just a little wheezier than they had been the day before. "A little tired, but okay." I nodded, and kept going.

The next morning's radio report from the Russian base camp was ominous. "A storm moving in," the thick voice intoned in a monotonic Russian accent. "Heavy clouds and snow. Perhaps several days. We recommend immediate descent."

"Oh, I don't think so," Scott muttered, and turned off the radio.

Wes peered out of the tent, past the liquid blue sky and out to where a few clouds were scuttling on the horizon. "There's something going on out there. But a week-long blow? Maybe not."

We had food and good tents; we could survive a long time on the mountain if we had to. We set our tents up on the Pip Plateau at 19,000 feet. As the sky grew darker and the wind whipped up and the storm bore down on us, we climbed into our sleeping bags and prepared to wait it out.

The storm kept us tentbound for three days. Finally it subsided, and we resumed climbing.

I got a slow start in the morning, leaving after most of the others had already packed their tents and taken off. Fredo had managed an early start but then stopped to rest. He was standing still just to the right of the footsteps kicked into the ice by the climbers ahead of us. Despite the exertion, his cheeks looked waxen, and I could see his chest heaving beneath his parka.

"You okay?"

It took a moment for him to answer. "Yeah." He breathed for a few more beats. "No problem. Go on."

"Sure?"

"Just a little tired."

We climbed to 23,000 feet, dug out platforms, and set up our tents on the ridge. By late afternoon we had started melting snow for dinner. Scott made the rounds of the tents to get out the word for the summit attempt. The wake-up call would come at two a.m., he said. Anyone who felt like getting up was welcome to go.

I ate dinner and then huddled in my sleeping bag. Exhausted from the day's climb but apprehensive about the coming morning, I sank into a shallow, restless sleep. Dipping in and out of consciousness, I swam in my sleeping bag, hearing the wind and loose snow blowing against the tent. I woke up briefly and glanced at my watch. It was just after midnight. Then I was asleep again, deeply this time.

I was dreaming the same dream I'd been having for the past three nights, ever since we were stranded on the Pip Plateau. It was an odd, frightening scene. I was on the mountain with Fredo, and he was suffering from pulmonary edema, a form of altitude sickness. He had rales, an edema-related condition in which his lungs filled with fluid, drowning him. Each gasping breath sounded like a death rattle. But I helped him down, my arm around his shoulder. I led Fredo back to base camp, and then he was fine. Each time it came, the detail of the dream was colorful and intense.

When I woke up, I was wondering: Was someone looking out for Fredo? I had watched him down on the plateau, faltering, but saying he was fine. A little sluggish, it was obvious, but Fredo knew about altitude. He'd climbed McKinley and Annapurna II. He didn't need baby-sitting. But something gnawed at me.

When Scott made the rounds of wake-up calls at two a.m., we all got ready at our own speed. Geo left first, then Scott and Wes. I was slinging on my pack and just about to leave camp when George

Kahrl leaned out of the tent he was sharing with Fredo and called me over. They were both in their sleeping bags.

"We're not going," George said. "Fredo's got rales."

My dream.

"Does he need help getting down?" I peered in at Fredo, huddled deep in his bag, panting lightly.

"Naw," George said. "He's not that bad off, and we've got enough people here to get him down to the plateau."

Fredo looked up at me and I waved. "How you doing?"

"Okay," he said. Fredo's voice seemed thick, but he was coherent. "I'm fine except for the rales," he rasped.

I gave him a long look and nodded. If Fredo said he was fine, then he was fine. "Okay," I said. I turned and headed up after Geo, Scott, and Wes. Mark Udall came a few minutes later, followed by Brad and Liz.

The others stayed in camp. Maggie was feeling the altitude again, a squeezing headache that sapped her strength and left her dreaming only of lower terrain and richer air. Mike felt the same; George, already thousands of feet higher than he'd ever been before, decided he too had gone high enough. The four of them would form at least two parties, and everyone would have someone else to descend with—Fredo especially, since he had the first signs of pulmonary edema. Someone would certainly be descending with him.

However, it didn't work out that way. Fredo left first, alone, telling George he was feeling well again. George followed, figuring he'd soon catch up and be able to watch Fredo the rest of the way down. Then Mike and Maggie left together. All of them were bound for our camp on the Pip Plateau, thinking they'd be there by late morning. By then the lower altitude would be easing Fredo's edema. Maggie and Mike would have clearer heads. If they had the energy, they might even go down farther.

But as dawn lit the sky, George couldn't spot Fredo. His tentmate wasn't on the route, nor was he waiting in the plateau camp. As morning turned to afternoon, George's concern took on an edge of panic. Fredo was missing. Maggie and Mike were also overdue.

The trouble started just after dawn, when Fredo left camp by himself. He was in worse shape than he had admitted. The ravages of altitude had fogged his judgment and stolen his sense of direction. What should have been a four-hour descent straight down to the plateau turned into a solitary nine-hour ordeal of wrong turns and desperate traverses. By the time he stumbled onto the plateau, Fredo was exhausted and barely coherent. And even after his 3,000-foot descent, his rales were as bad as they'd been that morning.

After putting him to bed, George sent out an emergency call. Soon an Austrian doctor and a few Russian rescue climbers arrived, but they didn't have all the medical equipment needed to stabilize him. All they could do for Fredo was to help get him down to base camp.

Meanwhile, the summit climbers had descended to the Pip Plateau. Scott and Wes went ahead to catch up to Fredo, while the rest of us remained behind to collect our gear.

While Fredo was descending, lowered on a rescue sled, his condition seemed to improve. His head was clearer, and when the rescue team hit some easier, flat terrain, he was able to climb out of the sled and walk. The group spent the night at camp one, at 17,000 feet, and as the night passed, Fredo gained more strength. He was rational, talking about his condition and eating and drinking. He was still shaky on his feet, however, and when they set out for base camp the next morning, the rest of the climbers took turns helping Fredo down the ridge.

Finally Scott began to relax. Fredo had had a close call, but the rescue had kicked into gear in time. They'd already lowered him far from danger—they were more than 6,000 feet from where he'd become ill, and even the most radical edema usually clears up after a 3,000-foot descent.

Three hours into the day's descent, Scott was taking his turn with Fredo, walking slowly with his arm around Fredo's shoulder. No need to rush now; they were only a few hours from base camp, and from there it was a short helicopter hop to the hospital. Scott was peering down the slope toward base camp when he noticed Fredo slowing down, teetering slightly.

"Okay, Fredo?" Scott looked over at him.

Suddenly Fredo seemed about to collapse. Scott grasped his shoulders with both hands, holding him up. Something squeezed

his heart, and he felt his own knees go slack. But he held on to
Fredo and tried to keep him on his feet.

"You can't stop." Scott said. "You've got to keep on."

Fredo shook his head. "I've got to."

Fredo sat down on the snow, then toppled over onto his side.
Scott looked down the slope and shouted for the others, walking a
few yards ahead. It took only a second. Fredo had been on the snow
for a heartbeat, but by the time Scott sank to his knees and rolled
him onto his back, Fredo had stopped breathing.

We were all incredulous. They had hustled Fredo down after
he got sick, literally thousands of feet beyond the point where an
edema should clear up. And he was improving! He was walking
and talking and doing fine, and then he just keeled over. But it
wasn't just his sudden downturn that puzzled us. How had he
gotten so sick in the first place? We could all see that Fredo wasn't
in top form when we got above the plateau. Whenever anyone
asked him, though, Fredo shrugged and said he was fine. At least,
until the rales kicked in.

But fatal edema rarely happens overnight. If Fredo's edema
was really that bad, he had to have been feeling awful for days. He
never told us, but we learned this for certain the morning after he
died. Someone had fetched his journal, and sure enough, the entries
started reflecting his problems two days after we left base camp:
"The hypoxia," he wrote, referring to brain-related oxygen depri-
vation, "is the best drug I've ever had." Fredo knew hypoxia was
an early sign of altitude sickness. Why didn't he tell anyone? Did
he really think it wasn't important, or was he too excited about
climbing the mountain to turn back? Was it his ego? Or did he just
assume he could get away with it?

Reflections

Knowing when to seek help. We've all heard it at one time or
another. I've uttered the words myself. "No thanks, I can do it

myself." Or, "I'm fine, thanks." And all the while I'm thinking, "I need help! No, I'm not fine, can't you see?"

At the beginning of his illness, Fredo obviously knew something was going wrong, but for whatever reason, he kept it to himself. When you conceal the truth from others, you eventually may be concealing it from yourself. The ultimate result is that you can get hurt, your teammates can get hurt, and your personal relationships and enterprise can get hurt, because you are trying to pretend that nothing is wrong.

When we pretend nothing is wrong, at work or in our personal life, instead of disappearing, the problems get bigger. We can't solve a problem until we face it honestly.

We have created a society where asking for help is a sign of weakness. Many men don't want to admit they're not macho; it makes them feel inadequate and uncomfortable. Women—especially if they feel in competition with men—may feel even more pressure not to appear weak. What would our coworkers think or say about us, if we admitted we needed help or didn't understand something? What would my climbing partners think?

Others, and I think women especially, fall into martyrdom. We take care of everyone else to satisfy our need to be needed, but we can't even admit to ourselves that we have needs too.

It is a sign of strength to ask for help. You may need to learn to lighten your load. People can get hurt the most, professionally or personally, when they think they can do everything alone. One key to achieving our goals is to accept our limitations and ask for help when we need it.

Most of the time, people love to be asked to help. They love to share their knowledge, their strength, and their experience. It gives them a sense of pride in themselves. When you ask someone for help, it sends the message that you value her knowledge.

This makes good sense. Why use up valuable time reinventing the wheel if there are others you can turn to? Not asking for help wastes time, energy, resources, and money. Asking for help increases teamwork, trust, and commitment.

Knowing when to offer help. When someone near you needs help but won't ask for it, you may sense it intuitively. Fredo's situation just didn't feel right to me, but I ignored my intuitive perception, and he died. It wasn't my fault, yet sometimes I wonder: What if I had gone down with him, as I did in my dream?

How do we know whether our intuitions are accurate? Often we don't. But it's important to pay attention to them. Certainly, we must enter and act on situations with solid information, but if for some unexplainable reason, the most obvious action just doesn't feel right, don't do it.

In your organization, do you have a structured approach to monitoring potential problems among your personnel that may cause harm to individuals or the team? Do you depend on individuals' intuition and informal reactions, or are you proactive in maintaining the physical and emotional health of team members?

It may seem obvious that we need to do this kind of monitoring in our personal lives; after all, that's where we learn the skills to begin with. Yet it's recently been brought home to everyone in this country that people may be neglecting the most basic responsibility to be sensitive to the situations of others: the parent's need to be aware of what their children are feeling and doing.

Keep a finger on the emotional as well as physical pulse of those close to you. It can be a matter of life and death: theirs, yours, or other people's.

7

Synergy

I lived in Seattle for two months, staying with my sister Wendy and her husband, John, and spending the days at Scott's office in west Seattle, helping to rope together gear and money for Everest. Even nine months before we boarded the airplane, we were already more than a year into our campaign to raise money, pull together equipment and food, and choose our last few team members for the 1987 American Everest North Face Expedition.

Our leader, Scott, had chosen the climbers for diverse skills that would be useful in both the planning and execution stages of the expedition. Resource tapping wasn't new to any of us. Most of us had some specific expertise beyond our climbing ability. Liz Nichol had solid contacts to food suppliers through her health-food business. Ben Toland was marketing director for Sierra Designs, an outdoor gear manufacturer. Attorney Geo Schunk could draw up contracts and help guide us through the federal tax system. Dave Black, an orthopedic hand surgeon, could be counted on to tend to sick and injured climbers once we got to the mountain.

Each climber had a specific area of responsibility in the preparatory phase. I was the equipment director, assisted by Evelyn, Rick, Mimi, and Melly. Liz and Bob were in charge of food; Geo and Peter were our legal counsels. Dave Black was our medical director, and Ben Toland and Q Belk were business advisors. Wes and Scott, as co-leaders, managed and helped out where needed.

Sometimes tasks dovetailed. When we decided to increase the number of American climbers in place of Sherpa staff to help us on the mountain, Scott made sure we increased the team's financial base by choosing new members who had money, or access to money and/or gear. Experience and climbing ability were still key factors, but other things could tip the balance of Scott's judgment. Peter Goldman, a twenty-nine-year-old appellate prosecutor in Seattle, had little mountain experience, but he did have quite a lot of money; before joining the team as a support climber, Peter signed over a check for $20,000.

As equipment director, I had to create two master lists of clothing and gear. The first was the group equipment list, which I computed from the top of the mountain down. How many tents would we need in each camp? How many sleeping bags, stoves, fuel canisters, pots? How much rope, how many ice pickets, ice screws, and carabiners would we need to connect the camps? I figured totals for dozens of other items to stock base camp: batteries, spatulas and silverware for the kitchen, tarps to cover boxes, hundreds of plastic containers to store food and equipment, a pump for kerosene.

Meanwhile, my second list tracked each climber's personal gear—everything from polypropylene socks to thermal underwear, wool mittens to thick pile hats. Toothbrushes, toothpaste, tampons, headlamps, ice axes, crampons, thermal sleeping pads, down climbing suits, harnesses, and thermoses.

Other people took a systematic approach, too. Using a typical business model, Scott, Wes, Q, and Ben came up with a detailed approach to funding and accounting. Everyone had a clear role, and expectations were well defined. Our communications were extremely well organized. We had a system to monitor our progress.

Every piece of our incredible pile of gear had to work. There's no point in hauling a stove to 23,000 feet if its fuel lines are going to clog there. With my detailed lists, I sent a questionnaire to each climber: What companies make the best gear? What brands or designs should be avoided? There was plenty of disagreement—climbers are an opinionated lot. Even so, compiling a wish list for fifteen of them was the easy part; the hard part was convincing manufacturers to give us the equipment free.

This is a standard ritual in the world of elite expeditions. Everything screams for big money—air fares halfway across the world, the local staff the governments require you to hire, the dehydrated food and high-tech clothing and gear. Scrimping on details isn't a good idea: there aren't any mountaineering stores at 25,000 feet. If you don't bring it, you won't have it, and not having it can mean forfeiting the summit, or even your life.

Our expedition budget was only $250,000; some groups spend a million dollars getting ready for Everest. And almost half our money would go to the Chinese government for permits and other bureaucratic expenses. Yet we needed $100,000 worth of equipment, and to stay within our budget, we'd have to convince manufacturers to donate at least 70 percent of our gear.

Collecting the quarter million in cash would be an even stiffer battle. As expedition leader, Scott took the lead in raising money, but we were all expected to pitch in. We were all keenly motivated: the more donations we raised, the less we had to find in our own pockets.

We made sure we looked professional. All the people we solicited received our pitch in a two-pocket folder imprinted with the custom-designed logo of the 1987 American Everest North Face Expedition. Inside, they found a color photograph of the mountain, thumbnail bios of the climbers, a fact sheet about the route, and the benefits of donating, with instructions on how to do it.

For just $25 a donor got a newsletter and the promise of a personal postcard mailed by a climber from base camp. A hundred bucks got all that, plus a photo of the climbers on the mountain. A replica of the summit flag came for a donation of $250. Any $500 donor received all that, plus a photograph of the actual load-bearing Tibetan yak temporarily renamed in the donor's honor and wearing a hand-painted plaque to that effect.

I had started targeting equipment manufacturers before we went to Pik Kommunizma. Scott, Ben Toland, and I went to a massive outdoor industry trade show, chatting up manufacturers. There were plenty of other climbers there for the same purpose. Tales of our upcoming journey to Everest got a good reception, and eventually we got $70,000 worth of donated equipment.

We also found the money we needed, thanks to a creative barrage of fund-raising. We held a benefit auction in Seattle with donated goods and services. We solicited small donors by promising to put their names on a strip of microfilm that would be left on the summit. We enticed larger donors by selling spots on a high-country trek through Tibet to base camp. We sold T-shirts.

By the end of winter we had recruited the balance of our climbing team. George Kahrl had dropped out. The final team included Scott, Wes, Wes's partner Melly Rueling, Q Belk, Geo Schunk, Dave Black, professional photographer Michael Graber, Ben Toland, Liz Nichol and her partner Bob McConnell, medical student Mimi Stone, and Peter Goldman. Given a chance to recommend climbers, I suggested my climbing partner Evelyn Lees and her husband, avalanche forecaster Rick Wyatt.

Later that spring we packaged the food and gear into portions, sealed it, and shipped it to Tibet. The boxes had to weigh 66 pounds or less, so our 30,000 pounds of food and equipment ended up as 460 wax-coated cardboard boxes, two feet wide, four feet long, and one foot high—the optimum size and shape for yak packing.

Six weeks before the departure date, we got together for a final meeting in Seattle. Scott led us through the details of the money we'd raised and our final tasks before leaving. In the end, he made one thing clear: when we got to the mountain, he wanted to stop being expedition leader. He'd still be the designated leader for official purposes and officiate in unraveling red tape on our way to base camp, but in everyday decisions about setting the route or planning summit attempts, he would wield no more authority than anyone else. We were all experienced climbers, after all; no one needed to be led by the hand. Most of us had known one another for years; we'd climbed together for years. If we couldn't run a well-organized, democratic expedition, who could?

That question would come back to haunt us.

Reflections

Whenever we are involved in a complex project, it's essential that everyone has a clear understanding of the project—that everyone knows his or her role and responsibilities. Because I knew everyone else was doing exactly what they were supposed to be doing, I wasn't burdened by worrying about someone else not doing a crucial job. This freed me to focus on my own responsibilities. A high-functioning team relies on everyone's taking responsibility for his or her own tasks, whether at home or in business.

In a nonthreatening environment, we worked well together. We clearly needed one another's skills and expertise. We created a synergy while preparing: our whole was more than the sum of its parts. We all knew that we needed one another in order to realize our dream of Everest. Open, clear communication was imperative. And the more we asked questions and got everyone's input, the more this strengthened the bonds of trust and respect we would need on the mountain.

My teammates and I were always asking one another for advice. How would you suggest I do this? What do you think? By including everyone in the decision-making process, we got buy-in. Even when someone didn't get his own way about a piece of equipment, he knew he'd been heard.

How are you creating this kind of involvement in your organization and in your home life?

8

Who Knows Best?

There's always something surreal about setting out on a long-planned journey. You think about it for so long, but so much work separates you from the trip. Finally, though, four of us gathered at Sea-Tac International Airport on July 22. The rest of our team would come later—we were heading to the mountain in different groups—but the departure of the first group marked the start of our climb to Everest.

The first Kathmandu-bound group included me and Wes Krause, his partner Melly Rueling, and Bob McConnell, a balding, bearded grizzly bear of a man. The four of us would organize the fresh food and buy other last-minute supplies. Scott Fischer, the expedition leader, and Liz Nichol, the food coordinator, flew directly to China to get the gear we'd shipped. The rest of our party—Peter Goldman, Evelyn Lees, Rick Wyatt, Ben Toland, Q Belk, Mimi Stone, and Geo Schunk—would meet us in Kathmandu four days later; two more members, Dave Black and Michael Graber would hook up with us at base camp.

Our plane descended to Kathmandu through heavy clouds and landed in a thick curtain of rain. We got our visas, collected our baggage, and passed through customs.

By now the rain was over. The sun pierced the layers of clouds and steam rose off the streets, dense with the ripe odor of the Third World. We walked out of the airport and stood on the curb for a moment, watching a knot of Hindu women swish past in their saris. The porters descended, coming in a swarm like feeding seagulls. The bus to the hotel was just across the street, but the porters—wiry men in blue cotton shirts—insisted on helping us from here to there. Eventually we managed to get everything to our temporary storage space, the back room of Yager Mountain Guides, a locally based guide service Scott had hired to ease us through Kathmandu and escort us through Nepal to our rendezvous at the Tibetan border.

After dumping our gear, we moved into the Kathmandu Guest House, an old colonial building. We spent the next few days filling in the gaps in our expedition supply list. Bob and I hunted down most of the fresh food, sitting in an open-air market to negotiate for garlic, potatoes, cabbage, onions, and mangoes. We also picked up bushels of canned fruit, spices, curry, salt, and sugar. We spent about $1,000 on the food, then started loading up on kitchen gear and some extra climbing supplies. We bought about 1,100 feet of Perlon climbing rope, several dozen propane/butane fuel canisters, and enough pots and pans to stock the main kitchen at Advance Base Camp. The director of Yager Mountain Guides helped us find two Sherpa helpers, Ungel and Renge, both experienced expedition cooks. Finally, we rented a bus to take us toward Tibet and hired a scout to work the road ahead of us, locating and hiring porters to haul our loads across the landslides that routinely blocked the road.

When Peter, Evelyn, Rick, Ben, Q, Mimi, and Geo arrived at the Kathmandu airport four days later, they found us ready to go. We'd finished all our chores: the fresh food was packed and waiting, the equipment was parceled up. Scott and Liz were probably settling accounts with the Chinese government even as we spoke and would soon be waiting for us at the Tibetan border. We were burning to get out of the city and start making tracks for the mountain. We would spend one more night in Kathmandu, we proposed, then start out in the morning. Our newly arrived friends gaped in horror.

"Are you nuts?" Q shook his head. "Come on, man. We just spent eighteen hours on an airplane. Don't we get a little downtime before hitting the road again?"

So we cooled our heels in Kathmandu for another thirty-six hours. Then we loaded the gear into trucks, and, early on the morning of July 29, set out for the Tibetan border.

The narrow road to Tibet heads up into the foothills, winding through the lush vegetation, past the terraced farms on the hillside beneath us, tall crystal waterfalls falling from the cliffs above, and a roadside chain of small, dirty villages, all ripe with the sour odor of decomposing garbage and human waste.

The going was slow. Every monsoon season unleashes a few mudslides over the road, and until the government highway crew repairs the damage in the dry season, auto traffic on the Nepalese highway is limited to the stretches between washouts. When we hit an impassable point, we hired porters to ferry the loads until another truck could resume the trip. Truck drivers who find themselves stranded between washouts can earn a good living working their own section of the highway, ferrying loads and passengers back and forth until the rock and mud are cleared away.

We drove only a few hours before we hit the first landslide, an enormous stretch of eroded highway near Llamasangu, a small village about twenty-six kilometers from Kathmandu. Our scout had already put out the word for porters, so when we stopped our truck, we were surrounded by dozens of eager villagers. Bob threw open the back of the truck and stood on the tailgate with our two Sherpa cooks, trying to distribute loads as fairly and evenly as possible. The throng grew and pushed close to the truck, a riot of chattering men.

Bob distributed the loads and gave marching orders to the troops, sending out fifteen porters with every two expedition members. We tried to be efficient, but with the constant negotiating and organization, the process used up the morning and then stretched into the afternoon. By the time the last of our ninety-two porters were sent up the road, the front of our expedition was almost two hours ahead of the rear.

Chaos reigned.

With the group trailing out over the hillside, our lines of communication dissolved. I walked near the back with Bob and Ben, and when we finally got started, we managed to travel for only half an hour before the daylight started to fade. We stopped for the night in an army camp in Langasangua. We didn't know where any of the others in our expedition were, and we found ourselves without food or a means of cooking. The three of us did manage to locate a box packed with cheese, which did for our dinner and breakfast. We caught up with the rest of the team the next morning.

Scott met us at the Tibetan border, and once we passed through Chinese customs we started up the road again, heading for the high Tibetan Plateau. When we reached Xegar, a small village with a military outpost, Liz was waiting patiently. There we spent three days resting and adjusting to the altitude. By now the land had turned barren and desertlike—a dry, windblown landscape, all dust and rocks and arid mountain air.

Soon our parade of trucks and climbers set out again, rumbling across the dusty roads, up the plateau toward the crooked, snow-covered pyramid we could now see ahead of us, above the mouth of the valley. Westerners call it Everest; its neighbors know it as Chomolungma, the Mother Goddess of the Earth. The sight of it! Just a few more days, I thought.

We rode in our slow parade, wearing masks against the dust, pile jackets against the chill, hats, sunscreen, glasses, and umbrellas against the strong rays of the sun. The cool winds are deceptive at 15,000 feet. Even bundled up, you have to remember to drink your fluids, or the sun and parched air will sap you dry within a few hours. We passed through a small town —small aggregations of low concrete buildings, some ancient stone ruins, a few tractors parked outside—and brought out crowds of townspeople. Small Mongolian-featured people, coughing from the smoke and dust they inhale all day, ears glinting with dangling turquoise baubles. (Tibetans see earrings more as an expression of humanity than as a fashion statement: either pierce your ears, or come back in the next life as a donkey.)

Traveling was easier on the dry, rolling hills of Tibet, but our road to base camp still had obstacles. Loaded into three rented trucks, we traveled only a day before one of them broke down. With the nearest replacement parts something like two weeks away, we unloaded our gear while Scott spent the next three hours negotiating with a farmer to use his tractor and trailer.

Late in the afternoon on our second day of travel, we came to a swollen river. When we asked our three truck drivers for their opinion, they advised us not to attempt to cross the river in the late afternoon, when the river was high with the day's snowmelt, but to wait until the next morning when the night's chill had slowed it. Scott was reluctant to halt: it was still early; we had several hours of daylight left; why waste it on this side of the river?

Finally our first truck driver took a deep breath and gunned his engine. He approached the river hesitantly. Slowly he inched into the water, which quickly crept up the tires. The water soon rose over the tires, and then he was stuck. He put the gears into reverse and gunned his engine. He inched backward, then switched into first and gunned it forward. It stopped in the same spot. He hit the accelerator harder and harder, spinning his wheels deeper into the boulders and rocks of the riverbed. The water was pouring through the cab. We were in trouble.

Our second truck tried a different route and strategy to get across the river. We got the high-wheeled tractor across and hitched a chain from it to the truck. While the truck driver gunned his engine, the tractor strained to pull it across. They made it.

The tractor went back for the stuck truck, but they couldn't budge it. By now half our team was on one side of the river and half on the other side. We didn't have a clue as to what we were going to do.

There was a village just down the river. Maybe someone had another tractor. It was worth a try. One of our truck drivers walked to the village. An hour later he arrived with a tractor. It took two tractors, another two hours, and a lot of money to break the truck loose and pull it to the other side of the river. By the time we got everyone to the other side, it was well past dark. And the stuck truck was barely working; water had gotten into the oil.

We rumbled into base camp late in the afternoon of August 8, unloaded the trucks, and bid good-bye to our drivers. Base camp on the Tibetan side of Everest serves mostly as a drop point for the trucks. The camp area is on the floor of a glacial valley, a flat, barren expanse between high, sloping walls of crumbling gray scree. The glacial moraine—the field of dirt and rock deposited as the front end of a moving glacier melts and runs off—is gray and dusty, like a high-altitude gravel pit. Close to 17,000 feet in elevation, base camp is a good spot for upward climbers to rest for a few days, pausing to adjust to the thin air while they double-check their gear. The day after we arrived, we spent hours organizing the equipment boxes—distributing personal gear, putting aside the things we wouldn't need for a while, setting up storage tents, and negotiating for forty yaks to carry the rest of the gear up to Advanced Base Camp at 18,500 feet.

It had been more than two weeks since the first group had landed in Kathmandu. We were poised to move onto the mountain. However, the expedition was still missing something—the distinct sense of togetherness that is needed to bond a group of individuals trying to collaborate. We still weren't all together. Dave Black and Michael Graber were trailing us by a few days. We'd been with Scott and Liz only for the days since we'd crossed into Tibet. As a result, the closest members were probably those who had been first to arrive in Kathmandu.

During our next-to-last dinner in base camp, Liz and I told the others we were thinking about making the forty-five-minute walk to the Rongbo Monastery the next morning. I'd been through the blessing ceremony once before, when I climbed Ama Dablam, and I think it's a good tradition to follow when climbing in the Himalayas. It shows respect for the local culture and puts the Buddhist Sherpas at ease. What's more, it gives the Western team members a chance to do something meaningful together before the climb—a moment for focus that transcends the relentless grind on the mountain.

But the response was silence. I looked over to Scott. If he decided to go, I knew he could get everyone else to go too. But he shrugged. "Go for it, if you want," he said.

And so our first attempt at building unity failed. In the end, our expedition never did quite come together as a team.

Reflections

Making haste. I am struck by the idea that this expedition which seemed to be a unified team back in the States, lost that quality once we left. We were always rushing to get here, to do this, to finish that. In our rush to get things done and get out of town we never slowed down enough to really bond. We found our endeavor fragmenting from the very beginning.

Our haste got us in trouble again at the river crossing. When you ask someone for advice, you might just want to listen and then follow it. The local truck drivers knew it was unsafe to cross the river at such a late hour, but we didn't listen. The people who are in the trenches know what's going on better than someone who doesn't do the job every day. Who knows the job better than the person doing it?

Maintaining communication. Once we got on the road, the front of our line didn't know what the rear was doing. The coordination we had enjoyed so much in our high-tech setting in Seattle fell apart. And no one was doing very much to remedy the problem.

What happens when no one takes on the leadership role? What kind of communication system do you set up when your team is extended, whether over geographic area or over multiple tasks?

Unifying a team. Keeping an endeavor on track, running smoothly, in a critical phase like this requires constant attention from someone charged with giving that attention. We had that in the United States, but things fragmented once we left. Without strong leadership, no one could confirm his or her expectations and role.

We were only organized to a point; after that, it started to degenerate into a free-for-all.

When a team or a group of people will be working together, there must be some way to bring them together before their work begins. Otherwise, people will just be working side by side, individually.

9

When Conflicts Arise

After a hearty breakfast of eggs, pancakes, and coffee, all fifteen of us set out in walking shoes, moving across the rocky glacial moraine. The yaks and their handlers—the "yaksters"—followed, carrying the gear to the spot we had established as our equipment cache. We walked alongside the bottom slopes of the Rongbuk Glacier, past the wall of ice towers built against the scree by the constant rolling pressure from above.

The yaks deposited our food and equipment boxes for camps 1, 2, 3, and 4 at the equipment dumpsite, a flat, safe stretch of the glacier about 45 minutes' walk above Advanced Base Camp. We would return again and again to the depot to pack loads up the mountain on our backs. We each picked out a likely-looking load and covered the remaining boxes with waterproof tarps. We donned our packs and our cross-country skis and started up the glacier for Camp 1.

It's an easy ski at first, up a few rolling hills and across a long gentle slope. After a while, the glacier arched higher, and we traversed the broad, steep snow face in a series of switchbacks.

From there we skied up to the right, heading to the center of the glacier in order to avoid the lip of the deep crevasses that ruffle the snow around the edges of the slope. We followed the glacier left, then skyward again, up a stair-step valley of slopes and plateaus. We stopped there, after almost two hours of skiing, and set up our first camp at 19,300 feet, a little more than 800 feet above Advance Base Camp, or "ABC."

We got to Camp 1 at midday and spent a couple of hours pitching the tents, stowing gear, and eating lunch. By early afternoon we turned back, skiing down the glacier to the edge of the dusty moraine. We spent the night in ABC, then repeated the process the next day—rising early to carry loads up to Camp 1, then skiing back down.

During the next few days the loads went up the mountain in haphazard fashion. When morning arrived, anyone who felt like going would eat an early breakfast and then set out for the equipment dump on the moraine. Once there, you could take anything that you thought needed to go up, load it in your pack, and then start for Camp 1.

Load weight and content varied according to the climber's opinion and mood. Most expeditions have specific load agendas; the expedition leader and base camp manager work together to ensure that the appropriate gear gets up the mountain at the appropriate time. But neither Scott nor Wes had bothered with constructing anything so formal. We'd already decided to work as a democracy, and we'd all climbed on big mountains before, so the attitude became "go with the flow." Everyone had the same goal; we all knew what had to be done.

In that spirit, while the rest of us were playing it safe and following the rule that it's best to not begin a climb with a massive altitude jump, Scott and Wes decided not to turn around the day we first established Camp 1. Their feet got itchy, standing on that snowy slope beneath the gleaming white North Face. Sure, it was only our first day above ABC. But with the sun beaming down and the breezes so light, you couldn't ask for better climbing weather. It was too perfect not to go. So, knowing that lines would have to be fixed to Camp 2 eventually, they headed off, hammering in three-foot aluminum ice pickets to anchor about 800 feet of line onto the lower reaches of the North Face.

Down below, we weren't really sure what had happened to Scott and Wes until they radioed down from Camp 1 just as the afternoon faded to twilight. "We're going to spend the night up here," they told us. Most expedition-style climbs move in small increments, like a caterpillar. You push ahead inch by inch, building a solid base of stocked camps and fixed lines as you go. Now, however, it was becoming clear that we'd abandoned any semblance of having a plan.

Here we were, our first day on the mountain, and already it seemed as if we were playing catch-up. Our co-leaders were gliding up the mountain so fast the rest of us had to hustle just to keep them in sight. We always seemed to be in a hurry, even when we weren't quite certain where we were going.

We stocked the lower camps through late August and early September, gradually carrying our entire store of food, gear, and oxygen to the supply stations at Camp 1 and Camp 2. In an expedition-style climb, the lower camps on the mountain serve as way stations for climbers and equipment headed up the mountain. On the North Face of Everest, Camp 1 sits just below the start of the steep part of the climb, the last refuge before the cliffs and avalanche chutes. Although Camp 1 was only 800 feet above ABC in elevation, the journey across the flat glaciers could take three or four hours and was exhausting under the scorching sun. Carrying loads from there up to Camp 2 presented a different series of problems, as the route turned sharply upward on avalanche-prone terrain.

We made dozens of trips during the first few weeks, until climbing the route onto the contours of the ridges and snowfields seemed as familiar as walking down the streets at home. But though the trek to Camp 1 grew into a routine, the climb to Camp 2 always put me on edge. To avoid the avalanches, we knew we had to climb up and down before peak avalanche time in the heat of the day. Sleeping at Camp 1, we'd set our alarms for two a.m., then switch on headlamps to climb in the dark.

We could ski for some distance, first up the steep slope directly above our camp, then on the gradual incline that leads to the avalanche cone—the accumulation of fallen snow and ice—at the base of the North Face. Then we'd set our skis into the snow a safe distance from the constantly shifting debris, put on our crampons, and start walking through the darkness, up the center lane of the avalanche highway.

The avalanche cone sloped up gradually, an open area directly beneath the throat of the Great Couloir. The chunky avalanche debris fanned out at the far end, growing more dense as it rose to meet the bottom of the couloir. Walking through the debris gave me an eerie feeling, particularly in the dark, when vision ended with the headlamp's faint thread and everything beyond was little more than a dangerous mystery.

If you imagine a couloir as being like a gumball machine, the cone is the slot at the bottom. It's almost inevitable that every avalanche in the immediate vicinity will run through it, and for the twenty minutes it took to climb the 300 feet of snow and ice I was on tenterhooks. In the darkness, the slightest breeze sounded like a roar. But the cone was our only way onto the North Face, the only conduit to Camp 2 and thence to the rest of the route. Every time I passed through, I crossed my fingers and tried to walk fast. And lightly.

The bergschrund, a three-foot slot in the ice wall at the bottom of the couloir, marked the top of the cone as well as the start of our fixed lines. At the fissure in the ice, we hooked our jumars—the ratcheted safety devices—onto the line, reached for a handhold, and hoisted up over the crack. Once on the slope, we kicked steps in the steep snow and ice, following the lines straight up the face for more than two hours, heading for a dark outcrop of sedimentary rock known as Greg's Gully. The lines ran straight up the vertical pitch. Once on top of the rock, we moved up a 200-foot knifeblade ridge, a long, steep climb overlooking the Great Couloir on the left and another deep gully on the right. The sun would be rising by then, shedding a thin morning light. Just above, the snow cave we called Camp 2 sat at the end of a flat section on the ridge, pecked like a woodpecker's nest into the bottom of the next vertical rise.

The familiar climbs could get tedious, but as I went back and forth I had a chance to climb with different groups. Each time, I was measuring my expedition mates' speed and skill—just as they were measuring mine.

Between ABC and Camp 1, I did most of my carries with Rick and Evelyn. After a decade of shared climbs I was already familiar with Ev's slow steady pace. She can handle anything in her own sweet time. Rick is a phenomenal athlete: a short fireplug of a man, all chest and pythonlike arms.

Ev can be extremely assertive in a social situation, but Rick can seem withdrawn. When he feels comfortable, though, he can hold forth not only on snow, but also on a legion of arcane philosophers, climbing trends, or obscure rock bands. While the other climbers were busy feeling each other out and trying to appear strong and impressive, Rick sat back with a passive grin on his face, listening.

But as the days passed, Rick didn't have a lot to smile about. While we were pushing our route higher on the North Face, both he and Ev were getting sick—a flare-up of his chronic intestinal problems and a bout of pleurisy for Ev. Weakened, both of them were quickly nudged to the background.

I could see it starting to happen one bitterly cold morning, on the route between camps 1 and 2. Climbing with Mimi, Michael Graber, and me, Rick could manage only a slow pace. Sapped by weeks of diarrhea, he lagged on the rock chimney, spending more than half an hour negotiating the brittle rock and ice. Meanwhile, we had to wait for him at the bottom, swinging our legs and clapping our hands to keep the blood flowing.

Mimi was beside herself. "What's his problem?" She shot a dark look up to Rick, still twenty-five feet from the top of the cliff. "I'm freezing. If Rick can't hack it up here, he ought to stay down below."

In a certain sense, I knew Mimi was right. Rick's strength was vanishing, and unless something miraculous happened, his time on the mountain was just about over. But the resentment flashing in her eyes revealed something else to me, too. Mimi didn't have any patience with weakness.

I could understand her frustration. I was cold too. But I'd climbed with Rick many times before, and I'd seen how fast and strong he is. Now he'd been weakened, but he was still trying. It was hard for the others to offer him the help he needed, though, because everyone was approaching the mountain with burning impatience. We had failed to form the bond that would have made empathy with Rick natural to us, and all we could see was that he was getting in our way.

Most of us carried full packs each day, lugging loads of food, climbing gear, oxygen bottles, and other essentials up the rock and ice faces. The climbing was hard, and building our camps wasn't any easier. Because the mountainside was far too avalanche-prone for tents, we had to dig out snow caves, each large enough for four or five climbers and all their gear. The work was an endless grind, and some mornings were difficult to face. But still, each evening brought a warm sense of satisfaction. We were one day closer to the top of the mountain.

And each day brought us one day closer to one another, but this wasn't always cause for celebration. At first everyone worked hard to be polite. As the expedition wore on, though, the veneer of team spirit started flaking away.

The first serious conflict came before Camp 2 had been officially established. The route to the camp was finished, and Scott and Wes had even put up a temporary supply tent. But we still hadn't dug the snow cave that would be the main residence, primarily because we decided it would be best to stock the camp without sleeping there. That way, we could build up our supplies above Camp 1 without depleting the food and fuel until we had to.

We all stuck to the plan for a week or so, until Michael and Mimi made a run to the second camp. Storm clouds had been brewing on the horizon since midmorning, and when they called down to ABC at noon, Scott had specific instructions: get down before the storm hits.

"No," Michael replied. "We want to acclimate up here for the night."

Scott stared at his walkie-talkie for a moment. "That's not exactly the plan," he said, frustration growing in his voice. "And you'll be up there a hell of a lot longer than a night once the storm blows in."

"That's okay," Michael's voice crackled. "We'll take the chance."

Scott threw up his hands. He hadn't come all the way to Mount Everest to spend his time screaming into radios. Michael and Mimi did as they pleased. In the end, they stayed up on the ridge for two solid days, eating the food and using the fuel as they worked to avoid the avalanches that threatened to sweep the tent down onto the lower Rongbuk Glacier. The avalanches got so bad that they had to dig the entire snow cave by themselves. Michael and Mimi came down looking chastened, but in the meantime, the maneuvering for summit position had started in earnest.

Without a strong leader calling the shots, each climber had to decide for himself or herself when to climb higher and when duty required a descent. Was the entire team going to dissolve into a loose federation of freelancers, or was Scott ever going to wield his authority to bring us together? If he didn't create some sense of team responsibility, how could we count on anyone getting to the top?

Insecurity bred defensiveness. No one knew the plan—we didn't have one. No one knew how the summit teams would be chosen, or who would be on them.

I found myself reacting to my teammates negatively, too. While I was resting at ABC one day, Bob approached me in the dining tent to ask if I could run a load of food up to Camp 1. I don't think I even looked up. "No," I replied.

A week before, I'd come down to Camp 1 expecting to find a fresh load ready to go up the mountain, but I found an empty supply tent. Furious, I called down to Bob on the walkie-talkie. "Where is the gear?" I shouted.

"What gear?" Bob's puzzled voice cracked on the flinty radio speaker.

"The stuff you're supposed to carry up here, so we can carry it up the mountain."

Empty static bristled through the small speaker. Then Bob's voice came back, tentative but patient. "What do you need right now?"

I sighed. "We need stuff, Bob. Stuff to carry."

"Well, what exactly?" Bob asked. "Food? Rope? Fuel? We've got it all down here. Just tell me what you need and I'll get it up to you—"

"All that stuff!" I shouted. "We're ready to make carries, but we need stuff to carry up the mountain!"

After weeks on the mountain emotional stress was running high.

Reflections

Monitoring and mediating. When a diverse group of people works together in a stressful situation, we have to accept the fact that there will be conflict. Minor incidents and problems, left unchecked, can escalate or balloon out of all proportion into major points of contention.

It is equally important to address and resolve conflict in personal relationships. If we don't do this at home, it can create bitterness and resentment. One partner may think everything is fine, while the other is angry and frustrated.

In an organization, this is where strong leadership comes in. The leader must be able to recognize and mediate conflicts before they get out of hand. What systems do you have in place to monitor and address conflict?

Balanced agendas. One out-of-balance individual can throw a whole team off. Soon a smoothly meshed machine turns into a clattering arrangement of eccentric parts, each adding its problem to the whole and exacerbating the problems of the others.

When I look back on this account, it's amazing to me now how petty some of our conflicts were. It's almost as if our team members were sabotaging the expedition. Instead of helping one another, we were hurting one another to advance ourselves. In fact, I am ashamed at the way I acted on this climb; in my desire to be the first American woman to get to the top of the mountain, I didn't care enough about my responsibilities to my teammates. Quite frankly, I didn't care who I stepped on to get to the top. This is a humbling realization about myself.

In life and in business, we do not get ahead by stepping on others: we get ahead by helping others and cooperating. If we had subordinated our individual agendas to the general goal, we might have worked together more effectively.

When we are involved in a team effort, it is almost inevitable that there will be someone on the team we don't like or admire. Nonetheless, we have to treat everyone with outward respect and courtesy. It is necessary to compartmentalize our impulses to express irritation with others and simply exercise common courtesy.

Clear roles. However good individual team members are at what they do, they must have their intermeshing roles clarified. I couldn't do my job of ferrying supplies because Bob didn't know what he had to do to make them available. Time was wasted; energy was not put to use; effort was duplicated. And because I had lost confidence in my teammate, I didn't feel the obligation to help him when he asked.

Expeditions don't just rely on each person to do his or her own task. We need to share information and thoughts to coordinate efforts. At certain points in an endeavor, certain team members will have to give more than their "fair share" in order to keep up the momentum. It's not just a nice idea—it's essential. We cannot achieve our goals by ourselves. It takes the hard work and effort of people working in cooperation to achieve anything of importance.

Necessary skills. While we were doing our individual jobs, working toward our common goal of Everest, our individual objective skills and expertise were assets. Once we got to the mountain, though, our lack of the other skills—interpersonal skills—caused our team to fragment. Hard technical skills are not the only necessity in an enterprise.

When I led my own expedition later, to K2, I paid attention to choosing people with the right character traits as well as the right technical abilities. What do you look for in choosing your teammates?

10

What's the Plan?

Fortunately, not everyone was competing in the summit sweepstakes. After a week of worsening intestinal cramps and congested lungs, respectively, Rick and Ev decided they were far too sick to risk climbing higher on the route. Ben also took himself out of the running.

By mid-September we had established our highest intermediate camps on the route—Camp 3 at 25,500 feet and Camp 4 at 26,500 feet—and then stocked them with equipment, food, and supplies. I began to wonder about our schedule. Without a solid chronology to go by, it was hard to tell if we were spending too much time stocking our route. How long would good weather hold out? How long would we be able to keep our strength on the mountain?

On an expedition with a strong central authority, the leader is free to build up the summit teams like a pyramid. Two or three of the strongest climbers get tapped for the first attempt on the summit, and the rest of the climbers work to support their journey. When the summit climbers are chosen, they return to base camp to rest; meanwhile, the other climbers stock the high camps, fixing the last portion of the route. When the summiters head up for the final push, their load is lighter and they can move that much faster.

But what happened at this ultimate stage of our expedition was almost chaotic. Michael and Mimi decided to make a summit attempt on their own; they were turned back by high winds a thousand feet from the top. Scott and Wes were going to make an attempt, and Q asked to accompany them because he was still healthy and strong. At that point, I felt my chances were slipping through my fingers; I had to do something quickly or I would never reach the summit. Even though the fragmentation of the team was making me feel like an outsider, I mustered the courage to ask Scott to join their party. And he said, "Sure!"

Reflections

It's inevitable that some climbers have to swallow their ambitions for the good of the expedition, but that's what expedition climbing is all about: you have to make a plan and stick to it as closely as weather and fate allow. If you fail to do this, you leave the door open for selfishness and failure. As the pressure mounts, an uncentered team can veer quickly into chaos. A group not bound to a plan is always one person away from total collapse—the moment one team member abandons the interest of the group, the others will quickly follow. It didn't take long for our group to cross that line.

On our expedition to Ama Dablam, things went smoothly according to Sue's plan for going to the summit. Everyone got to the top, in the predetermined order. This was partly luck, of course—no one can count on favorable high-altitude environmental conditions. But it was a relief for all of us not to be in suspense about when and with whom we would make our summit attempts. With less guesswork, we had more energy to focus on our tasks.

How are you prepared to manage the unexpected—to function effectively in chaotic, turbulent times? Is there a plan you can turn to?

11

Lighten Up

That afternoon the blizzard slammed into the face of Everest, but we hardly noticed. Tucked in our warm little L-shaped snow cave, we were completely insulated by the translucent snow. No matter how violent the tempest outside, we could barely hear the wind, let alone feel it. The temperature outside may have swooped to 30 or 40 degrees below zero, with the wind-chill factor, but our cave stayed a pleasant 32 degrees above. As the wind screamed and the snow flew from the heavy black clouds, we sat up in our sleeping bags, drinking hot chocolate and chatting merrily. We fixed dinner as the daylight faded, then snuggled in for the night. In the dark I lay daydreaming and waiting for morning. By then, I hoped, the skies would be clear and we could return to our route, kicking steps to Camp 3, then to Camp 4, and then up to the summit.

When we woke the next morning, Q and I found that our sleeping bags had been dusted with snow that had floated in through the tunnel. While we brushed it off, Wes peered up into the tunnel. His peering space was severely limited. The entire tunnel, we discovered, had been filled with snow. This presented several problems, not the least of which was the fact that the tunnel opening was our only oxygen source. Wes grabbed a shovel and started digging. After half an hour he managed to clear the passage, but when he came back he had snow stuck in his black beard. We learned we'd be staying put for at least another day. "Snowing like a bastard out there," Wes announced. Though we could barely hear it, the wind was ripping across the mountain like a freight train at more than 100 miles per hour.

It was snowing so hard that when Q bundled up to take a look for himself fifteen minutes later, the tunnel Wes had just cleared was already clogged. Q dug out the passage again, then used four ice screws to hang a tarp at the front entry, protecting our enclave from another onslaught of spindrift.

It'd been a hard morning, but during our ten a.m. radio call we learned how easy we had it in our cave. During the night, Bob told us, Advanced Base Camp had been buried under four feet of snow. "And the wind's howling down here. You guys may be up there for a while."

When Scott put away the walkie-talkie, we sat back and listened for the storm. All we could hear was the muffled rumbling of an avalanche. Wes cocked his head and wrinkled his brow. Outside in the tunnel, our tarp wasn't even flapping.

"Awful quiet, don't you think?"

The fallout of another passing avalanche filled our entrance.

When you're riding out a storm in a snow cave, life boils down to a matter of time. Without books, cards, or any intellectual diversion, the minutes and hours assume their purest form. Sleep is the only shortcut, and after a day or two even that comes slowly. Depleted by the climb, squeezed by the altitude, and cramped by the limited space, the abused body turns surly. At altitude the digestive system chokes, muscles atrophy, and any kind of movement taxes your resolve. My back and shoulders were stiff from endless hours of lying down. My hips ached from hours of sitting.

I wanted desperately to move.

Through two days, then three, then four, the black clouds hung low over the mountain. Just outside our little entryway, the arctic wind screamed like a jet engine, lashing the curtain of heavy snowflakes nearly horizontally. Later we'd learn that we were sitting through the most violent snowstorm to hit Everest and the Tibetan plain in more than forty years. Until it was over, we had no choice except to stay cavebound.

In a snow cave, it takes a lot of time just to survive. Cooking and eating can take up hours of the day, and at altitude it's always good policy to take on calories. But it's a physical reality that the human digestive system never absorbs 100 percent of what you eat. Waste builds up in the bladder and the bowels and eventually must be eliminated. In a crowded snow cave at 23,500 feet, in the midst of a violent snowstorm, this can present a problem.

Even though we were not exerting ourselves physically, we still needed to drink seven to nine quarts of water each day. At this altitude, you are constantly drinking, day and night. At night you sleep with two one-quart bottles, one filled with water and the other empty. Every time you wake up, you take a sip from your water bottle. By the time morning rolls around, the water bottle should be empty, and the empty bottle should be filled.

We were all accustomed to using pee bottles in our tents at night. Just use the bottle as you need to, then go outside in the morning and dump the contents into the snow. Most people can pee in semipublic circumstances. As long as you don't spill anything, or get your bottles mixed up, it's not too traumatic. But try moving your bowels in public.

"I am not going to poop in this cave." Scott made his intentions clear at the end of our first day of captivity. After years spent playing and working in the wilderness, Scott had no problem relieving himself in the out-of-doors, even in the harshest conditions; wandering off alone into the bushes or behind a tall ice tower can actually be sort of relaxing. But doing it surrounded by people in an enclosed space was something else.

That was fine. After all, it was only the first day.

After our breakfast of mashed potatoes, butter, and instant coffee, Scott again announced, "I'm not going to poop." I didn't quite understand why he felt he needed to make a public announcement.

On the third day, Q, Wes, and I started taking bets on just how long Scott could hold out. Well, after five days on the mountain, you either poop or get off. Inevitably, Scott had to join the rest of us in once a day exchanging his pride for the physical reality of being a human organism.

Even if you take to it more easily than Scott did, bowel movements in close company are still an unnerving process. Begging everyone's pardon, you reach for a Ziploc plastic bag and ask the others to turn their heads. Nonetheless, the progress of the act is usually painfully obvious to all. Odors tend to carry and linger. And the pressure of altitude seemed only to increase flatulence. We stored the plastic bags near the front entryway, where the contents would freeze.

Reflections

What worked under sunny skies no longer worked in a snow cave. We had to develop an entirely new set of ground rules for this process of elimination. If we didn't figure out a system in the beginning, the time in the snow cave was going to be extraordinarily trying. We communicated about our new system, but one of us couldn't bring himself to accept it. That created tension among all of us.

Sometimes a person lets his concept of the way things are supposed to be get in the way of dealing with the way things really are. Scott's notion of propriety and his belief in his capacity to control his body were at odds with the reality of our situation, and he ended up causing himself pain.

Learn to laugh at yourself. Often, when we're in the midst of an intense situation, we take not only the situation but ourselves seriously. However serious the situation may be, when we take ourselves too seriously we can become ineffective. We narrow our field of vision, our options. Our egos get in the way; we become self-conscious; what people think of us matters too much.

If we lose our sense of humor in crisis situations, we become weakened by the crisis. It doesn't even need to be a crisis: if we can't keep our perspective when little things happen, those little things will wear us down and weaken us.

Laughter, or even quiet humorous reflection, releases tension and stress. When we lighten up on ourselves, we relax and become more, well, creative.

12

The Limits of Survival

On the morning of the fifth day in our snow cave, the clouds finally broke and the sun rose into a clear sky. Stepping outside the tunnel for the first time in ninety-six hours, I could finally look out into the world below. The snow was everywhere now. Even the Tibetan plateau, once brown and gray, was covered by a thick blanket of pure white. The wind was still blowing, but it wasn't going to sweep us off the mountainside. Not down at this altitude, anyway. Up above, the summit was still trailing a long plume of spindrift. But for the time being we were okay. And most important, the horizon was crystal clear in all directions.

Still, before we continued up the mountain we had to consider how our bodies were responding to the altitude. We'd spent the last five days above 19,000 feet. Deprived of oxygen, there was no way our digestive systems could assimilate enough calories and nutrients to keep our muscles intact. Our bodies were slowly wearing down.

I could feel it as soon as I climbed out of the cave and stood up. I struggled to draw a breath; my knees felt rubbery, as if I'd been going hungry for days. We all felt the same way. But after all this time and all our work, this was our only shot. We went back inside to pack our gear and get dressed, and Scott called down to Bob at ABC.

"Are you sure?" Bob's voice crackled.

"Absolutely," Scott said.

We retraced our steps up the ridge, through the rock shelf and then White Limbo. Everywhere the snow was hard and crusty, packed down by the wind. The gale-force gusts had faded, but without the cloud cover, even the moderate winds were searing cold. My layers of polypro and down did little to warm my toes, and I had to stop regularly and swing my legs back and forth to keep the blood flowing.

On the White Limbo the days of gale-force wind had rendered the slope almost unrecognizable. The windpack had formed sastrugi—an eccentric pattern of uneven ridges and fins. Where the mountainside had once been smooth, the snow now swerved and undulated. We followed our ropes through the ridges for 300 feet. Then Scott turned around and shouted down to us.

"The ropes are gone!"

When I caught up with him, I saw it too. Our rope, once connected to the mountain by three-foot ice pickets, had been ripped completely out of the snow and ice. Now the lines were lying 150 feet away, strewn against the ridges in the snow. From where we were standing I could see that the ropes were still intact, but the metal stakes had been torn out of the ice, one after the other, twisted like licorice whips.

Unroped, I walked more slowly despite the cold. I was thinking about those metal pickets, twirled like string by the force of the wind. I was feeling even greater respect for the mountain and the vast forces of nature.

We climbed the rest of the way to Camp 3 without our fixed ropes. As we got higher, the wind started to gust more strongly. When it blew up, I'd have to brace myself on my ice ax, leaning down into the slope. The sastrugi made it difficult to find solid footing. I had to watch each step, leaning on my ice ax and planting my crampons with care. We arrived at Camp 3 about two P.M.

The storm had also plugged the entrance to this snow cave, so we spent the next three hours digging our way in. This entry presented a more complex dig than the cave at Camp 2. Because the serac hid a crevasse, we had to go a long way to find snow solid enough to support our cave. In the end, the tunnel stretched fourteen feet, swerving left, curving right, then sinking down again into the cave itself. As the smallest in our party, I had to do most of the digging, lying flat on my belly. When the tunnel sloped down, Q had to stretch out behind me, holding my ankles.

Once we managed to squeeze inside, we fired up the stove to melt some snow for dinner. Beneath the pot the flame sputtered; like human bodies, stoves prefer to work where there's more oxygen.

I was exhausted from the day's climb, but that night sleep came hard. The cave was frigid because the long, diving tunnel worked as a cold sink. Whatever insulation the snow provided was negated as the heat flew up and out, and cold air from outside settled down on us like a blanket. And now that we were above 25,500 feet, the altitude squeezed that much harder. Lying perfectly still, muscles relaxed, I could feel the weight pressing against my temples—the pressure of oxygen depletion. I slept fitfully, feeling the months of hard work and harder high-altitude conditions, bones poking through my skin, sore hips and shoulders.

Still, we all woke up the next morning eager to climb higher. We knew we were getting closer. If our luck held, we could get to Camp 4 by this afternoon. Then, when the sun rose tomorrow, we could climb out of our tent and head for the summit.

We ate quickly that morning, shoveling in the oatmeal with grim determination. No matter the weather, we had to keep making progress. If we found ourselves beaten back by the wind, we'd never be able to get back up again. We were already behind schedule, thanks to the snowstorm. The Himalayan autumn was waning, and our window of opportunity was sliding shut.

I wriggled into my layers of down and then crawled through the tunnel, pushing my pack out ahead of me. I saw daylight ahead of me, and the instant I poked my head outside the cold air burned my eyes. The morning sky was clear and bright, and a cruel wind swept past us. Scott had gone out ahead, and I found him standing by the entrance, struggling with his crampons. I looked over at him.

"Brr!" My voice blew away in the gale. "Kinda cold out here."

Scott looked up. He'd stripped down to one layer of gloves to set his crampons, and the arctic cold was giving him fits.

"My fingers are freezing."

He slithered back into the tunnel to finish setting his crampons out of the cold. Meanwhile, Wes crawled out of the tunnel, slung on his pack, and adjusted the straps. He looked over at me. "Ready to roll?"

We went together, traversing around the front of the serac, then making the abrupt turn where the route continued upward. That's where the wind caught us full in the face. We both looked up at the same moment and saw the summit.

A dense curtain of snow was blowing out into the sky. The cloud of spindrift was so thick it made Everest look like a volcano in full eruption.

"It's gotta be a hundred miles an hour up there," Wes said. When we ducked back behind the serac, Scott and Q were walking toward us. Scott flashed a smile.

"Let's do it!"

We shook our heads. Scott's smile faded.

"What's wrong?"

Wes pointed around the serac, up to the summit. Scott and Q went around to look. A few minutes later they came back.

"A little windy," Scott said. "You don't think we can make it to Camp 4?"

Wes shook his head. "Once we get a little higher, I don't think we could even stand up."

I nodded. "We'll have to sit it out until tomorrow." When I caught Scott's eye, he screwed his face into a sour look.

"Shit." Scott stepped back around the serac and looked up again, as if maybe this time the winds might have died, and the summit might look more inviting. Still the deadly white banner flew from the top of the mountain. Scott pulled at the straps on his backpack, then walked back to the cave. "Tomorrow," he said, "we're going up this mountain."

Another day in the cave. We sat in silence, lost in our own thoughts. We'd worked so hard, for so long. We felt fine, even after our week in the snow caves. But here we were again, turned back for another day. After all this time, no one had the energy to be angry. For a long time, no one said a word. A gust of wind blew a small shower of spindrift through the tunnel, and it fell like hope- lessness, into our hair, across our faces, down our necks.

Drinking coffee a half-hour later, we grasped a thin thread of hope. The weather could be better tomorrow. The winds couldn't last forever. "We're too close," Scott said. He set his jaw. His blue eyes turned hard and steely. "There's no way we can stop now."

We were so close. From where we were sitting, curled in the dim light of a snow cave, the top of the world was only 3,000 feet away. Less than two days of climbing on the jagged north face of Mount Everest. But we weren't climbing.

We were hiding. It was late in the climbing season, and the winter winds had descended—for how long? Sitting up in my sleeping bag, balancing a cup of hot coffee in my lap, I could imagine that the hurricane outside would vanish. In the dim light of the cave, I could overlook the heart-squeezing pressure of life at 25,500 feet. I could almost convince myself we wouldn't have to turn around when morning came.

Turn around? Not after I had devoted years of my life to get here. Years spent dreaming of scaling this massive hill and then leaving my footprint on the crown of the earth. The years of planning, hundreds of thousands of dollars, commitment from people some of us had never even met. We had to get to the top. No matter what you say, it does come down to black and white: the expedition either touches the summit or comes home ready to explain what went wrong. Now we were two-thirds of the way there, 25,500 feet up the North Face of Everest. Stranded in a snow cave, yet so close.

But determination goes only so far. You have to recognize the true limits of survival, to know you can push yourself only so far without disaster. It's a corollary of the conscious decision I came to during the storm on Mount Robson: the choice between life and death. We had to stop. After the long day and one more freezing, endless night in the snow cave, we crawled outside only to find that the winds above were blowing even harder.

We crawled back inside the cave and sat again in silence. We were all absorbed by our own thoughts. Do we go up or do we go down? Do we pursue our goal adamantly, regardless of the consequences? Or do we retreat altogether, with only the hope of someday, some other time, reaching the top of Everest? No one wanted to be the first to say "Let's go down." So we just sat there. The silence was as cold and oppressive as the weather outside.

Finally Q spoke: "If I don't go down now, I don't think I'm going to make it off this mountain."

That's all we needed to hear. It takes strength and courage to climb a mountain. It takes strength, courage, and wisdom to turn around.

Reflections

Knowing when. Even though we may rarely face situations that threaten our very lives, each one of us has to make decisions in our personal, family, social, and business lives. And each time, it's crucial that we know when to proceed, and when to give it a rest. Timing plays a critical role in succeeding. Knowing how is the easy part; knowing when is difficult.

Nine years later, in 1996, news media around the world were riveted by the drama of a group of climbers trapped in severe weather near the summit of Everest. Among the parties in trouble was a group of inexperienced climbers led by experienced guides. It was extremely difficult for the guides to let their clients down when they had promised them the summit. When failure is not an option, our thinking can become narrow and clouded, and we can take unwarranted risks to succeed. In this case, that cost eleven people their lives, including my good friend Scott, who was one of those guides. Be careful what you promise: your promises could end up hurting everyone.

There are many things you can't force. You have to pay attention to your environment, whether it is dominated by the forces of nature or by the manmade forces of economy, politics, and society.

There is so much pressure to succeed, to get it right the first time. Sometimes we continue to push harder and harder to figure it out, to solve the problem, to make things happen. But sometimes, the harder we push the more resistance we encounter. When we're under pressure and stress, it can obstruct or blind our thought processes.

Retreat and regroup. We had not envisioned a retreat from the summit attempt. We were prepared and highly motivated. But we were stopped by something beyond our control. Doesn't this happen in our personal and professional lives too? We come up with a strategy, map out our route, and think we are doing everything right, but then some external factor forces us back off the mountain. We have to cut our losses and figure out another way. If we stay alert to changes in our situation, we can adapt and change course.

It's important to learn to back off, to ease up, to release the pressure and stress. Then we gain new perspectives, so that we return to our effort refreshed. As we huddled over our decision, high on the north face, we were not devoid of consolation, because we had hopes of trying again someday.

Reframing failure. Have you ever thought about the difference between giving up and defeat? It lies in our ability to respond to the outcome. I've written about giving up—resigning oneself to dying or living in misery. There is no learning drawn from giving up. Defeat, in contrast, is often only a temporary condition. When we respond positively to a temporary setback, we analyze and learn from our mistakes, so that we can go back and try again.

I like what Pat Riley, the famous basketball coach, said: "There are no failures, only results, so get busy doing what you can to make the results better."

Fear of failing can be fuel for achievement. However, you can't make yourself a victim of that fear. There came a point when our determination not to fail became counterproductive. We were fortunate that we could reach down deep enough to find the wisdom to recognize that.

The more creative or experimental your endeavor is, the more it requires openness to failure. Accept it as an essential part of the process. Look for the lessons in it.

The ability to maintain one's self-confidence in times of adversity is largely determined by one's capacity to reframe failure experiences. Failures that remain unexamined eat at the spirit and will of any person.

A clear vision. We all have to adjust to setbacks, and we must be prepared to try again if we want to climb our mountains. Dwelling on failure is counterproductive. At this moment, all of that is in the past. Instead, look to the future. Ask yourself: "What specifically did I do to contribute to the setback? What can I do to ensure a better result the next time I try? And what did I learn from the experience?"

My setback strengthened me. Now, more than ever, I wanted a shot at climbing Everest. I left Everest feeling as if I had unfinished business. Setbacks can be motivators. Instead of bleeding away energy regretting and worrying over the past, we can harness that energy to accomplish our goal the next time.

What does it take to get back on the mountain again? How do you overcome the depression and frustration of having to start over again? When you get knocked down, a clear personal vision will start you on the road back. My personal vision was to stand on top of Everest. It was clear, concise; it was where I saw myself. I was extremely disappointed when I didn't get there, but I didn't give up because I had a vision of where I saw myself.

What is your vision? Where do you see yourself? Commitment to that vision of who you are and where you want to be will provide the strength, courage, and resilience to try again.

Ama Dablam (22,495 feet).

Dave Hambly just below Camp 3
(23,700 feet).

Stacy rock climbing in Russia.

Dave Black just below
Camp 2 (23,500 feet).

Q Belk and Stacy in the snow cave, Camp 3
(25,200 feet).

North Face of Everest
above Camp 2
(23,500 feet).

Advanced Base Camp after a storm
(18,500 feet)

Mt. Everest (29,028 feet).

The 1998 Everest Climbing team: Larry MacBean, John Petroske, Shirley (Jean's girlfriend), Don Goodman, Jean Ellis, Jim Frush, Stacy, Steve Ruoss, Diana Dailey, Bob Singer, Charlie Shertz, Geoff Tabin, Peggy Luce, Dave Hambly.

A mountain of gear.

At the end of the Puja, the blessing ceremony, with bits of sampa smeared on our faces and hair: back row, Charlie Shertz and three Sherpas; front row, Dawa, Geoff Tabin, Steve Ruoss, Stacy.

Base Camp, 17,600 feet.

The Khumbu Ice Fall.

Diana Dailey crossing a ladder in
the ice fall.

Carrying loads under an
overhanging serac in the ice fall.

Avalanche in the Khumbu Ice Fall.

From Camp 2 at 21,500 feet, looking up Lhotse at our route, which goes just left of the jumbled ice in the center, crosses the ice face, and goes up to the left ridge at 26,200 feet.

Camp 3
(23,700 feet).

Pasang Gaylsen and
Stacy on the summit
of Everest.

Summit Ridge.

13

A Sense of Self

I had always pushed myself. Growing up, competing with my sisters and brother, I always strove to be better: to ski better than I ever had, to get better grades, to swim faster. Part of that compulsion was healthy: I wanted to see what I was capable of doing, to see if I could reach a horizon beyond the one ahead of me.

In the early days of my first marriage, I felt my husband, Mark, and I could do anything. I thought we had perfect synergy. But then things changed. I grew dependent on him. Eventually my dependence submerged my own strength, and I felt strong only when I was with Mark. I was blind to his own weakness, and I followed him into an orbit where I became too weak to hold onto my own sense of reality. When the violence started, a pattern was set: we were locked together, beyond reason. By the time Mark slapped the divorce papers in my hand, my sense of self had been whittled away.

I staggered through the weeks after Mark left me, even sinking so low, one gloomy night, that I found myself thinking about suicide. It never went beyond a thought, but it was a chilling moment. Seeking strength, I had been emptied of my own, and now I felt so worthless that I could even imagine, briefly, that I'd be better off dead. At that moment, I knew I wasn't contributing anything to life, and I couldn't see what life held for me.

Except the summit of Everest. The First American Woman. By the time I got to Tibet, that title represented everything I thought I needed: a new identity, a new sense of self. So when we were turned back by the winds, the fact that I hadn't taken those last few steps onto the summit overwhelmed every other step I'd taken on the journey. When I looked ahead, I could see only the top of Everest.

Having failed, I stopped and reassessed my reason for climbing Everest, and I found that reason lacking. I had been driven by the desire to become the first American woman to climb Mount Everest. During the climb I was only focused on the summit, on being first. I believed that the incidental fame that would come with the accomplishment would solve all my problems.

Before, I had been climbing for purer reasons—the challenge and excitement, the beauty of the wilderness and the friendships that grew there. Curt and I didn't climb the Cassin Ridge to impress people or earn a place in a record book. We chose the harder route on Mount McKinley because it posed a physical and mental challenge.

Remembering that helped me realize that I don't climb for fame. I discovered that it's not enough to believe in my goal. I also have to believe in the reason I'm doing it. Had I not failed, I might never have experienced such revelations about my own motives. When I had to reframe my failure, I realized that self-esteem is built from within, not from some external achievement.

I also realized that even though I didn't get to the top of Everest, it was an incredible opportunity. Consumed by the drive to the summit, I temporarily forgot about the incalculable privilege of being one of the few to climb on such an extraordinary mountain.

When I let myself believe that one title would change my life, I lost sight of my true reasons for climbing. That's one reason I later found it hard to commit to my next Everest expedition in 1988: I couldn't bear to push myself for what I feared were the wrong reasons. It's not enough for me to believe in what I'm doing; I also have to believe in my motivation. Now I had to come to terms with the truth: personal triumph does not come from winning a race. The real triumph is when you can accept yourself in any weather and in any state, and still be able to say, "That's me, and I'm okay."

For me, that meant more than coming to terms with my own sense of climbing. I also had to make sure I understood how my climbing affected the other people in my life. Mountain-climbing is an exceptionally selfish sport, after all. Going after a big peak means making a stiff investment in time, money, and risk. You're gone for months, in the most remote, often dangerous parts of the globe, in subzero temperatures, freight-train gales, murderous snowstorms, with tomblike crevasses spiraling beneath your boots, perhaps just beneath the thin crust of powder snow your foot is about to break through.

Imagine how it feels to be the one left at home. Waking up in the middle of the night, reaching over and feeling the cold half of the bed where your mate should be. Or as a parent, wondering where your daughter is, if she's safe. When the telephone rings late at night, you take a deep breath before answering. You never know what you might hear. The other side of the bed may never be warm again.

I had always heard rumblings from my family. "It's so selfish of her, going off to climb, and God only knows when or if she's coming home." Couldn't I see what I was doing to them?

David thought about it seriously when we started dating. I was preparing for the second expedition then, gradually putting everything else on hold. He saw me getting excited, conceivably preparing to walk off the face of the earth, and he had to ask himself: "Do I really want to fall in love with a woman who does things this dangerous?" In the end, however, he accepted the risk.

I understood the selfishness involved. I could see how hard it would be for my loved ones to watch me walk back into the unforgiving realm of steep ice and rock. But I needed my family's support. Before I left, I needed to know that they understood why the mountain was so important to me.

I did know one thing for certain: if David ever told me not to go—it's me or the mountain, take your pick—I would immediately have chosen Everest. As much as I loved David, I wasn't about to change my life again to suit a man's purposes. Fortunately, I never had to make that choice. David understood me better than that.

He could see it from the first time we went rock-climbing together. It's an intense focus, he says. A clarity in my eyes that I get only when I'm climbing. My voice gets higher, the words are more animated and flow faster. It's almost as if I'm in a trance, I seem so completely connected to what I'm doing. It's something deeper, something he wasn't about to try to unwire. "I know it's important to you," he'd say. "I'll be here when you get back."

But what about my family? I had already sensed my sister Wendy's disapproval: "Isn't once enough? Why do you need to go back?" And I had long assumed that my mother felt the same way. When I first started rock-climbing and venturing off on expeditions, she never held back her opinions. Why did I have to center my life around something so dangerous? At first she made a point of telling me why she didn't like my climbing. I ignored her, but even when she stopped talking, I always assumed she was thinking it anyway.

I underestimated her. She had grown to understand why I climbed. She said, "Of course you should go back to Everest. Climbing is how you express yourself."

Before the British mountaineer George Leigh Mallory died on Everest in 1924, someone asked him, "Why do you want to climb Mount Everest?" He responded with an answer almost Zen-like in its clarity: "Because it is there."

It sounded so brave, so daring. You could almost see the shrug of his shoulders, the steely glint in his eye. "Because it is there." It had the ring of manifest destiny. "Because it is there," Mallory said, and those words have defined all those who climbed after him. The battle was joined, and once again man would emerge victorious. He had seen, gone, and—of course—conquered.

But that's not why I climb.

I climb because I'm here.

I don't battle the mountains. I don't conquer anything, even when I do pull myself onto a summit. For me, the triumph now comes in every step, in every breath and heartbeat. It's the sheer pleasure of being on the planet, of seeing the mountains around me and, for a brief moment, being part of them. My spirit leaps, my voice joins the chorus of the living. I climb for a simple reason: because I'm alive.

And that's why I went back to Mount Everest.

14

This Is a Team

Before I even returned to the United States, a new route opened up to my goal. Scott contacted the leader of the 1988 Northwest American Everest Expedition and recommended me. I was interviewed by the entire team, and three months before they left the States, they asked me to join them.

The expedition included thirteen Americans and twenty-six climbing Sherpas. Our leaders were Jim Frush and Don Goodman. Besides me, there were two other women, Diana Dailey and Peggy Luce. The other climbers were Steve Ruoss, Charlie Shertz, John Petroske, Dave Hambly, Jean Ellis, and Geoff Tabin. We also had two base camp managers, Larry MacBean and Bob Singer.

At the airport the day we departed, there was electricity in the air—along with lights, cameras, boom microphones, and reporters armed with pens and notepads. Almost by accident, our expedition had become something of a civic event. A year earlier, Jim had called the Seattle Times in hope of landing a cash donation. The publisher passed on the sponsorship deal, but then he called back with an offer just as valuable: "Why not let us turn your climb into a series of stories?"

Seattle had a bond with Everest that stretched back twenty-five years to the day when hometown boy Jim Whittaker set foot on the summit. The Northwest's climbing population had exploded since then. Taking a step-by-step look at a modern expedition vying to put the first American woman on top would be a great way to update the Whittaker story, while at the same time engaging outdoorsy Northwesterners.

The Times assigned the series to recreation writer Sherry Stripling, a former sportswriter. Sherry, a trim, athletic woman who had even tried out an ice ax and crampons, sat in on a few meetings and cranked out her first article, which focused on our drive to collect equipment. It touched a chord, particularly the part about our need to find free clothes: "Underwear for forty people adds up," Jim was quoted as saying. "And we like to change it occasionally." Sure enough, Times readers flew to our aid, though not perhaps as we had hoped: several readers sent in pairs of boxer shorts.

Sherry wrote a dozen more articles before we left, and by the time she came to see us off at the airport, she was tailed by a whole gang of broadcast and print reporters. We held a short press conference. Jim introduced all climbers, thanked a few of our larger sponsors, and read a statement of our objectives. Coming back alive, he said, was everyone's first priority.

After a few questions and answers, it was time to leave. A camera or two followed us to the gate, along with a few friends and family members, all waving and shouting for good luck as we boarded the plane and took off into the deep blue sky.

We spent two nights in Hong Kong and went on to Kathmandu. Once settled, we spent a few days shopping for fresh fruit and vegetables and a few last items of gear. Jim and Don, meanwhile, spent most of the next eleven days locked in the Nepalese Ministry of Tourism, negotiating the tariffs and import charges for our gear.

None of us had come to Kathmandu intending to hang around for eleven days, but we tried to enjoy ourselves. We started each day with a communal breakfast, meeting at a small teahouse. Diana and I shopped for food and looked for trinkets and clothes in the open market. She was full of energy, always moving and taking notice of the world around her. I spent an afternoon with Steve Ruoss. Tall and laconic, he did his share of the chores, then spent the rest of the day exercising or exploring the city with Geoff Tabin. I got used to Geoff's boyish sense of humor.

I also had a chance to spend more time with our teammates who were based on the east coast. Larry MacBean, a middle-aged businessman from Maine, brought a well-honed sense of order to his role as base camp manager. Charlie Shertz, a thirty-four-year-old anesthesiologist from Pittsburgh, was a sporty guy, and Bob Singer was accustomed to a more staid existence than he was finding with us. A sixty-year-old neurosurgeon from Richmond, Virginia, Bob had not worked too hard at being physically fit, but our trip changed his life. To prepare, he started lifting weights and hiked the entire Appalachian Trail. He was our other base camp manager.

Reflections

We started out as a team way back in the States. There was never a point at which we lost communication and went off on our own tangents. By getting to know one another, we were building a commitment to help one another when it became necessary.

Later that commitment would pay off. Even though there were the inevitable conflicts, we were able to get past them because of two factors: strong leadership, and the foundation of trust and respect we had built.

15

The Trek

We finally left Kathmandu on the morning of August 5. After loading our 450 boxes into a truck, we piled into a small bus and set out to Jiri, the small hillside village at the end of the road. The morning was warm and wet, the heavy breeze full of flowers and mud and the odor of rot—half-eaten vegetables scattered on the road, garbage piled on the sidewalk, human waste in the ditch. The bus rumbled up the road, lurching across each rut and bump, gradually climbing higher into the emerald mountains.

Unlike the Tibetan side of Everest, the west side has no road for vehicles beyond Jiri. The path is steep and rough, a stiff up-and-down climb, gaining 30,000 feet and losing 15,000 in the space of 125 miles. It usually takes more than two weeks to trek into base camp. Tucked into a dingy guesthouse in Jiri, we went to bed early, planning to rise before dawn and get a fast start on the path to Everest.

We were traveling during the monsoon season, and the lower part of the trail was muddy and slippery. The hot, muggy, rainy weather kept us in shorts and T-shirts. That made us prime targets for the predators that lurked in the dense vegetation: the leeches.

In Nepal, leeches are the national nuisance. During the monsoon season they're everywhere on the damp jungle hillsides: small, brownish slimy creatures hanging on to the vegetation, waiting for the next unsuspecting warm-blooded creature to come brushing past. Once on board, they go to work, scuttling to a likely place and then attaching themselves with their pronglike fangs. Then they inject their natural anticoagulant and start sucking up blood, engorging themselves and dropping off without raising a tickle.

The bites aren't dangerous; they don't hurt or itch, and they rarely get infected. But it's so gross! If you happen to notice some on you, in the act, you can snatch them with your fingers and try to pull them off. This is complicated, though, by their stretchy bodies, which can go on forever like a rubber band, and their sticky skin. Once you've succeeded in pulling them off your leg or arm, it's another disgusting job to get them off your fingers.

If you don't happen to notice the leech in the process of leeching, you probably won't feel anything while it's there. After it's dropped off, however, the leech's anticoagulant is still working, and then you feel the warm blood running down your leg.

Reflections

Do you have leeches in your lives? There are some people who can suck us dry without our even noticing. We've probably all been around "needy" people who leave us feeling exhausted; they've drained us emotionally. Or they may be so negative that they erode our positiveness.

We must learn to pay attention to how people affect us. It can require conscious attention to remain enthusiastic in the presence of someone who constantly finds fault and makes excuses. If you can, spend as little time around these people as possible; if your profession forces you to associate with them, learn to distance yourself emotionally.

We can also sap our strength by trying to control or change others. We cannot really control other people, or change other people; we have control only over ourselves—our own responses to others.

Leeches are the uncontrollable things on which we spend too much time and energy. We must learn to focus on the things we can change and the things we do have control over, and let the other stuff go.

We couldn't control the leeches. Every time we turned around or removed one, there were more waiting to pounce. We could choose to spend energy worrying about the leeches and getting upset, but it wouldn't make any difference. Choose your battles wisely; spend energy only on what you can control.

16

Celebrating a New Endeavor

When we arrived in base camp on Mt. Everest, we met up with most of the Sherpa climbers who would help us carry our loads of food and equipment up the mountain. Our Sherpa staff were all Buddhists. Before they climb any mountain, they perform a Buddhist blessing ceremony, a puja, to ask the gods for guidance and a safe return. Our Sherpa staff invited us to be a part of their puja.

A few of the Sherpas spent an afternoon building a six-foot stone altar on the edge of our camp. They erected a pole in the center to serve as a central stringing point for our one hundred meters of prayer flags. The flags, strips of cloth inscribed with prayers, flutter in the wind, and the winds carry the prayers to heaven.

The next morning we climbed out of bed early and gathered at the altar for the puja. The Sherpas were already there, chanting and burning juniper branches for good luck. We each made offerings to Buddha, arranging them on a shelf on the altar. The Sherpas laid out sampa, or balls of barley flour. The American climbers offered what we had—M&Ms, Fig Newtons, and rupees (Nepalese money).

The chanting went on for close to two hours, rising in wild crescendos, then falling to a murmur. Occasionally they'd call us to throw handfuls of rice into the air, as another offering to Buddha.

We didn't comprehend the religious significance of the ceremony as the Sherpas did, but it gave us all a chance to feel joined in a team effort, to reflect on the mountain and challenges ahead of us. When it was over, we all threw barley flour in the air and smeared it on one another's face and hair. The white streaks represented a long, happy life. And with the ice fall just ahead of us, we were especially eager to wish for long lives.

Reflections

This ceremony was a powerful communication tool. Through it, the Sherpa staff communicated with us about something deeply important to them. It helped create an atmosphere of understanding, and thus of trust. It was an act of cooperation, of inclusion instead of exclusion, and a celebration of small victories along the way to the big one. It also gave us the opportunity to come together as a team, to refresh our spirits and refocus our energy on the mountain.

Participating in rituals, even if these are not religious or even traditional, increases solidarity in the group. Our culture lays great emphasis on celebrating major victories: the achievement of the summits. But if we also recognize and celebrate the smaller, daily successes along the way, it refreshes our spirits and gives us renewed momentum.

Children and their families recognize small daily successes. This builds the children's self-esteem and confidence and gives them their own momentum to attempt new tasks.

Recognizing people makes both sides feel good. Seeing others' joy makes the spectators happy, too.

17

Working with Other Teams

Once we got out of base camp, our immediate problem was figuring out how we were going to work with the seven other international expeditions on the mountain. Even when we arrived at base camp and found only the Koreans ahead of us, we knew that in the space of two weeks, the camp would swell into a small international village. It didn't take long for the relations among the eight teams to develop UN-style convolutions.

The biggest challenge involved the path through the ice fall. There would be eight unrelated teams following the same route through the ice fall. Obviously, no one team should have to provide all the raw material and effort to build the path. We had anticipated this while planning our expedition and, trusting at least one of the other teams to do the same, we had brought only about two-thirds the number of ropes and ladders required for the route. The team of South Koreans had made the same bet, and so once we met up at base camp, we soon struck a deal to pool our resources and manpower to put the route through the ice fall.

Once we came up with a working plan with the Koreans, Jim Frush, our expedition leader, divided our team into three rotations, each group going up to work on every third day. The alarms went off a two a.m., so that the bulk of the day's work could take place well before the midday sun heated and loosened the ice from the surrounding peaks—before avalanches threatened. After a quick breakfast, the first group donned their backpacks and headlamps, met the Koreans on the edge of camp, and set out through the darkness. On the first round, I got to sleep through the wake-up call, but my day would come soon enough.

The ice fall is part of the Khumbu Glacier. The glacier flows like a very slow river; at the point of the ice fall, it cascades over a cliff for two thousand feet, just as a waterfall would drop. It continues to move downward at approximately three feet a day. When a solid moving mass of snow and ice drops like this, it breaks apart, forming huge ice towers and huge slots called crevasses. Because it's constantly moving, it's constantly changing. The ice towers can tumble down without warning, existing crevasses become wider, new crevasses open up, and it's not uncommon for entire sections to cave in on themselves.

You can never forget about the movement, because you can hear it. It's creaking and moaning beneath your feet. You can sense intermittent vibration and, now and then, the shifting of the living ice.

Every climbing season, a new route has to be put in through the ice fall. The previous season's route has been either disassembled or destroyed by the movement of the ice fall. Setting the route can take anywhere from six days to two weeks—an eternity spent zigzagging around impassable ice towers and seeking out natural ice bridges to cross the crevasses. What can't be avoided must be bridged, so we brought along seventy-five aluminum ladders, each of which had to be carried into the ice fall and then hoisted over or across the obstacles. Each ladder could span an eight-foot gap, but when we encountered something larger or wider, we had to rig the ladders together, connecting the spans with rope and custom-built metal clamps.

Each day in the ice fall was spent playing an obscure, dangerous game of trial and error. We met the Koreans at three a.m., then walked across the glacier to our equipment depot at the foot of the ice fall. There we paused to strap on our crampons. We clipped onto the rope and started up past the ridge of ice that marked the entry to the ice fall. From there we followed the rope through its tangled path, up to where the previous day's work ended.

By now the sky was paling with dawn, and the texture of the ice began to throw shadows in the dim light. We preferred to move as quickly as possible. We wanted to be safe in the ice fall—not making any impulsive judgments, always taking time to do the right thing—but we all knew the problem with that. No matter where you were inside the ice fall, you'd be about a thousand times safer if you were anywhere outside the ice fall.

Crossing the ladders required the utmost focus. Ladders were never really meant to be laid horizontally. If a crevasse is spanned by one ladder, there's no noticeable flex in the ladder when you cross. One crevasse, though, started out as a five-ladder span, and by the time we left the mountain two months later, it had opened up to an eight-ladder span. Through most of the expedition, we were not able to anchor the ends of these ladders on the sides of the crevasses; they were several inches or a foot from the sides, and the entire ladder was suspended from fixed ropes. It was like walking a tightrope.

The first time I crossed the five-ladder span was on the way out of the ice fall after a day's work. My crew had put it in. Instead of hoisting it over the crevasse, we had to climb down 60 feet into the crevasse and up the other side, and then pull the ladders across. On the way out I paused and looked around. On my immediate right, I couldn't help but notice the ten-ton ice block poised above me. Then I looked down at the bottom of the 60-foot crevasse I was about to cross.

My heart pumped wildly, I took a deep breath, and then I took my first step. Only a small bounce at first. Then another step, a little more shaking. Just focus, concentrate on each step, don't look too far ahead, one step at a time. You can do it. Ice block, sixty feet, crampons, tripping.... My mind raced. Each step toward the center of the span was shakier, and the ladders began to do what they're supposed to do: flex. By the time I reached the center, the ladders had sagged at least two feet. As I got to the other side I thanked the ladder gods for sparing me. Several members of our team opted to crawl across.

The Koreans had a very different climbing style than the Americans. They were much more aggressive and took more risks, often walking around unroped, almost barging ahead without thought to safety. We were much more conservative and tended to want to talk about options, about our safest route. Learning how to work with our different styles was hard. But it was the balance between risk-taking and conservatism that got us through safely and quickly. The Koreans helped us establish the route a lot quicker. We helped the Koreans stay safe.

Reflections

Facing the fearsome. There's no way around the Khumbu ice fall: we had to go directly through it. Fear is our growing edge. You must go through it to experience the power of overcoming it. Until you have the courage to cross the ice fall rather than detour around it, you will not experience the higher awareness and fulfillment that lies on the other side. Every time you cross a ladder, you will build more confidence for the next one.

Fear grows while we postpone action. To fight fear we must act. Our obstacles become surmountable if, instead of cowering before them, we make up our mind to walk boldly through them.

Sometimes starting out can be the most challenging and frightening part of an endeavor. But once we actually begin, our momentum builds and we grow more confident. It certainly is easier to stand outside our icefalls and look at them, but we discover what we're capable of doing only after we take that first step and negotiate the difficult, frightening terrain.

Questioning decisions. Climbers must be constantly vigilant toward one another's decisions and actions. It's dangerous to make assumptions. It was important for us to ask questions and double-check anchors and route location in the ice fall.

It is also dangerous not to question in business. Everyone has the responsibility to question the decisions being made around them. Questioning is a matter of safety. What can you do to help create an environment where people are comfortable and encouraged to question the decisions and actions of others?

Keeping plans flexible. Even though we could see the entire ice fall from base camp, we couldn't map out our exact route from base camp. We had to start into the ice fall to find our way around the myriad ice towers and crevasses. Sometimes we found ourselves proceeding in the wrong direction. After climbing, anchoring our ropes and securing our ladders over crevasses for hours, we'd come up against an impassable tower. We'd have to backtrack, taking out the ropes and ladders we'd just laid, and find another way around.

When we have a vision, a plan, we usually cannot map out our exact route. Our external environment may be imperfectly known, or it may change so rapidly that we cannot make a plan that takes every eventuality into account. We have to stay alert and adapt from moment to moment. Sometimes we have to back up, count our losses, and figure out another way to reach our goals. In a changing environment, we have to be alert and flexible to adapt constantly.

Maintaining focus. Focus, or concentration, is the ability to be present in the moment. Going over the ladders in the ice fall, you focus on one step at a time—not on the sixty-foot drop below you or the ten-ton ice block looming over your head.

Sometimes we become so distracted by what's going on everywhere around us that we do not focus on our immediate responsibility. Learn to tune out distractions and keep focused on objectives.

Using diversity. Not everyone crosses the ladders the same way. Some people crawled across. Each person has a unique comfort zone and must decide individually how he or she is going to do things. It didn't matter that people did it differently, as long as it got done.

Some organizations want all their people to do things the same way: this is how we do it. Often this stifles creativity. When we have the freedom to try things differently, it fuels our creativity and stimulates us to come up with better, more productive ways of doing things. The styles of the Korean and American teams on Everest were different, but this difference benefited us in the end: the route went up faster than the Americans might have achieved alone, and it was safer than the Koreans might have made it.

Studying others. Each year expeditions put a route through the ice fall, but each year it is destroyed by the movements of ice and avalanches. We could not follow the previous expedition's exact route, but we did use their experience as a resource, to help us construct our route. In life, we cannot follow another person's exact route, but we can use their experience to help us in ours. Talk to people; read biographies. Don't imitate others, but respect their experience.

18

Strength out of Adversity

The ice fall made me feel like a deer during hunting season: very alert and skittish, always ready to bolt. It was so beautiful in there—the jagged towers scraping the air, frozen clear in the dawn, the rising beams of morning sun playing on the sparkling ice. But I was always aware, ears open, eyes wide, toes feeling for the slightest vibration, the rumble in the distance. I saw everything and ignored nothing.

We made group decisions and tried to be as logical as possible. Which was the biggest threat: avalanches, ice towers, or crevasses? One morning we took a moment to consider this. We were about a third of the way up the ice fall, poking around for a route beneath the West Shoulder of Everest. If we set the path closer to the mountain, we could avoid a long line of crevasses and some huge ice towers. But being closer to the hill also meant being closer to the avalanches that sometimes came roaring down 1,500 vertical feet from the overhanging glaciers.

We stood for a moment in the pink light of early morning, our breaths coming out in white puffs. We searched one another's faces, then headed toward the shoulder.

We got used to the sound of avalanches. The crack of release, the dull rumble as the snow and ice spills down the slope. Some avalanches are larger—and louder—than others, and you look up when you hear a big one start to go. But even in the ice fall that morning, below the overhanging, snow-covered cliffs, that one sharp snap didn't faze anyone.

I'm sure I heard it, somewhere in the back of my mind. Crack! Then the low rumble. But we just kept working, pounding in the ice pickets, threading the rope and moving up, while the avalanche came rolling down, a dull growl at first, then louder. It built into a solid rumble, then a roar. At this we looked up. A cloud of white billowed up as the avalanche loomed down the slope, steadily gaining size and momentum. It was coming closer to the ice fall. And it was headed straight for us.

Now we all saw it. A blue bolt of fear shot down my spine. Now it was louder, the white plume growing wider and closer. In one movement, Jim and I unhitched from the line. The two Sherpas working alongside us did the same, and we all scrambled away, searching for a safe spot.

As the roar grew even louder, I could feel the ice beneath me tremble. There was nowhere to run. Crevasses were everywhere. We finally found a small ice seam to hide behind.

I pressed my chin against my chest and braced myself, anticipating the impact, the wave of snow sweeping me off my feet, spinning and pummeling me, burying me. I could feel the blow, the cold wash of the snow, the blank white as it consumed me—and then it didn't come.

Instead, the rumbling lightened, then stopped. I felt a cold wind rush over my head—the air displaced by the wave of snow and ice. Then silence. I kept my head down for a few moments. When I looked up, a thin cloud of ice particles danced in the air, sparkling white against the blue morning sky. The snow had slapped against a small wall of ice almost a hundred feet away—and stopped.

We all stood then, tentatively. We dusted off the ice. "That's it," Jim said. "Let's get back to work."

That afternoon in base camp, Don said he felt very uncomfortable with placing our route so close to the West Shoulder. He was concerned about more avalanches and was adamant that we move the route. That would have meant a lost day of work in the ice fall. A lot of work and effort had gone into anchoring our safety ropes and laying the ladders over the crevasses. No one wanted to go back up and take our route apart and start over.

So far, we had done almost everything by consensus. Now Don was challenging that consensus. We discussed it for hours, and everyone else thought the route was fine where it was. Finally Don said, "Okay, I still don't feel good about it. But I'll go along with the group's decision to leave it where it is."

The next morning at base camp felt wonderful. I slept until five-thirty, then woke up on my own. There are so few luxuries on a glacier at 17,600 feet, but this was mine: lying in my sleeping bag, waiting for Jetta, our thoughtful cook, with the mug of hot tea he brought to help ease our way into the day. I lingered even longer, feeling the tea settling into my stomach, radiating heat all the way into my fingers and toes, warm and relaxed.

Then I heard the explosion.

It was a bomb. It registered deep in my sternum. I vaulted out of my sleeping bag, pulled a jacket over my long johns, and stepped into my boots. I didn't pause to lace them. I scrambled out of my tent and jerked upright, searching the mountainside.

A huge one...but where? In the tent next to mine, Charlie was leaning out, his long black hair still tangled with sleep, steam still rising from the tea mug in his hand.

"Avalanche!" I shouted at him.

I didn't have to shout. Now we could see it clearly, even from a distance. A huge white cloud was billowing from the West Shoulder, the biggest I'd ever seen, sliding down toward the ice fall. Two tents away from me, Dave Hambly leaned out in his underwear, camera pressed against his face, shutter whirring.

We watched it together, faces slack with helplessness. Don, Peggy, Diana, Geoff, three Sherpas, and at least that many Koreans were up there setting the route. But where? All we could do was watch the snow and ice tumbling down the slope, hitting bottom and rolling into the throat of the ice fall. Across the route! And then it was quiet again.

Jim, standing in his long johns and a down jacket, stared up toward the ice fall. When he broke his trance, his eyes flickered, then hardened.

"Let's get a rescue going."

He turned and walked toward the Sherpas who were standing outside their tents. Charlie, in unlaced boots, dove back for the tent he shared with Jim, pulling out the base camp walkie-talkie. After an avalanche that size, Don would certainly call down. Outside I could hear Charlie, his voice high-pitched, yearning.

"Base camp to Don. Come in, over."

Nothing. Just a click as he pushed down the button and tried again. "Base camp to Don. Looked like a big one up there, let us know what's happening, over."

Charlie stared at the radio in his hand, then gazed up to the ice fall again.

"Base camp to Don. Give us a shout, okay? Looked pretty big."

All we could hear on the walkie-talkie was the caustic scrape of radio static.

Up in the ice fall, the first warning had come half an hour before: a sharp crack from above, then a small white cloud rolling down from the ice cliff on the West Shoulder. Working on the route, Don glanced up at the avalanche, then quickly back to the line he was setting into the ice. No big deal.

The snap twenty minutes later was even smaller. Don was deep into his work by then and he didn't even look up to trace the path of the ice down the slope. The climbers were spread up and down the line, Don working most closely with a young Sherpa named Kami, pounding in ice pickets, feeding the line through the carabiners. Moving up another ten, twelve feet, then doing it again, whacking away at the picket, planting it good and solid in the ice, clicking on a carabiner, then snapping it around the line.

That's what they were doing, standing in the middle of the most exposed stretch of the route, when they heard the noise above them. Kaboom! This time it sounded like a cannon, only louder. It got everyone's attention.

To Don, it looked like the entire ice wall had broken away. He watched it fall for a moment, saw it hit the slope and blow apart. The force of impact took out a chunk of the slope, and the slide gained momentum as it rocketed down the steep hill. From below it looked as big as a tornado, and it was blowing right toward them.

Don craned his neck. He knew he had about six seconds, maybe eight. An eternity to think in, but too little time to move. And where would he go? There was nothing, not even a lip of snow, to lie behind. All he had protecting him, Don realized, was the slim rope and the skinny pickets they'd just spent the last two hours pounding into the ice. Don motioned to Kami and clipped both of them back onto the line, and they huddled together. The ice beneath their feet shook. The thick white cloud of ice particles loomed above, swallowing the pale morning light. Don and Kami turned sideways to the onslaught and hunched over, making themselves as small as possible.

Don could feel Kami trembling. "Cover your mouth!" Don shouted over the roar. Kami nodded, and then he could hear Kami praying. Don cupped his hands in front of his mouth.

Then it hit.

The cold wind ahead of the avalanche tore Don's hands from his mouth. His hands flew away, and then he jerked sideways, feeling the fixed line strain behind him. The first wave of ice came in the cloud, a hail of sharp fragments that sliced skin like razor wire. The next wave of debris consumed them both, pitching Don and Kami backward with enough force to tear the fixed line away from its three-foot pickets. Uncovered, Don's mouth sucked in a thick cloud of ice particles. He couldn't breathe. He was somersaulting, pitched like a rag down a thirty-foot ice cliff.

So this is what it's like to die in the Khumbu ice fall.

But then it stopped. Don's eyes were closed. He wasn't sure where he was now. Wasn't sure if he was now. All he knew was the hollow silence, the cold, something dripping off his chin. He was dazed, but alive. He was okay. A little banged up, but still—he heard moaning.

Kami.

Next to Don, only Kami's face emerged from the snow. The brown skin was battered and torn by the ice. Mixed with melting snow and hot tears, the blood dripped pink. Kami tried to move, struggling against the weight of the snow. He groaned again, and Don reached for him, cradling his head in his arms.

Then he heard a voice echoing from above. Don looked up and waved. The others made their way down, carefully, crunching in the rough ice, and reached for Don's arms to pull him out of the snow. Don motioned to Kami.

"I'm okay. He's worse."

The silence was eternal. But ten minutes after Charlie first tried to rouse him, Don finally answered.

"Everyone's alive."

There was something in Don's voice. A catch. Something wasn't quite right.

"Yeah. Looks like, maybe we're gonna need some help getting down."

Everyone was alive, thank God. But both Don's and Kami's faces had been sliced, diced, and battered by the fragments in the ice cloud. Don netted a broken finger and a black eye during the fall. Kami suffered the same cuts and bruises, and the impact against the ice had torn ligaments in his knee. The others in their party had barely been knocked over by the tumbling debris.

We were relieved to see them all, to have everyone back safe and relatively sound. After years of hearing the horror stories and tales of sudden death, we'd finally been touched by the ice fall's brutal power. But we were lucky this time.

Reflections

Moving beyond blame. Don was the one member who wanted to move our route farther away from the West Shoulder, and, ironically, he eventually was hurt because we didn't move it. It would have been easy for Don to come back down to base camp and point a finger and lay blame for his injuries on us. The way he handled this event could have been very divisive for us. If Don had been angry, if he had said, "I told you so," he would have created defensiveness, guilt, and bitterness that would have been tough to overcome. But he didn't.

So often, as we react to errors, we blame other people or circumstances for what happened. Spreading blame just adds to the already existing distress when a mistake has been made. It can blow up a mundane error or complaint into a crisis—perceived, if not actual! People who have been made the targets of blame become worried and insecure; they may become unwilling to take independent action for fear of further blame-laying. Can the people around you risk making mistakes because they are secure in the knowledge that errors will be corrected without blame-laying? How have you been reacting to mistakes? Do you learn from them, correct them, and move on calmly?

Don is a true leader. When he arrived back at base camp and doctor Jean gave him his clean bill of health, he almost immediately began to strategize where we would move our route to make it safer from impending avalanches. Don accepted the results of the group decision and moved on from there.

We clearly misjudged the avalanche potential of the route. We learned from our mistake, and we spent the next day reconstructing our route in a safer location. True leaders do not blame other people or circumstances for their lives. They take full responsibility. They learn from mistakes and use their new knowledge to move on. Only when we take full responsibility for our lives will we have the confidence and courage to take risks. By taking responsibility for himself, Don was able to move beyond blame and muster the courage to continue upward.

Responsibility for one another. We learned a lot more from the avalanche, of course. We learned, at a gut level, what we already knew intellectually—that we were all vulnerable there on the mountain and that we were all responsible for one another. So all of a sudden we had a strengthened purpose: to watch out for one another. Our team spirit could have died in the Khumbu ice fall; instead, it came out stronger than before.

19

A Clear Plan

Once the route through the ice fall was set, we were heading up the mountain. Assuming the weather didn't turn vicious, this was the last night we'd all spend together on the glacier at base camp. From now on, most of our healthy climbers would live on the mountain, helping to set the route and establish the camps, then ferrying gear up to stock the higher points.

Shouldering loads, we set out the next morning for Camp 1. Almost everyone turned back for base camp that afternoon, but Charlie and Geoff spent the night at Camp 1 to acclimate, and the next morning they started fixing the route up the gently sloping Western Cwm (a Welsh word, pronounced "coom," meaning "valley") to Camp 2 at 21,500 feet. Once established, that camp would become our mountainside headquarters, while Camp 1 served as an equipment depot.

Work on the route started before dawn and finished by midday. Down at base camp, Larry and Bob would parcel out the food and gear that needed to go up the mountain. Then the climbers would carry the loads up through the ice fall, leaving the gear at

Camp 1. Once the loads were at Camp 1, we'd climb down from Camp 2 to pick up the gear and take it to the camps above. As always, the acclimatization strategy was one step up, two steps back; climb higher during the day, drop off a load, and then retreat to a lower camp to rest for the night. It was a conservative approach, but it lowered the risk of altitude sickness and helped us stay strong.

When the assignments came out in the morning, I strapped on my crampons and went where I was told. Some days I got to venture high on the route; other days I stayed low, humping loads up from Camp 1. The cwm was riddled with crevasses at the bottom, but after a few hundred feet of switchbacks and traverses to avoid these, the glacier became solid again and the climb more direct. From there it was a long, flat walk up to Camp 2. Above that camp the glacier sloped gradually for another quarter mile. Then our route slanted right, heading straight up the Lhotse Face to Camp 3, four small tents dug into the steep mountainside at 23,700 feet.

We had been climbing for fifteen days when I made my first carry to Camp 2. At Camp 2 you finally feel like you're on a mountain. In the deep valley you are surrounded by Everest, Lhotse, and Nuptse. From Camp 2, I could see where the rest of our route would be located. As I gazed up toward Camp 3, then Camp 4, though I couldn't see the top of Everest, I could see the summit of Lhotse at 26,000 feet. It was a long way up there, and Mt. Everest was another 3,000 feet higher. I was a little overwhelmed and discouraged. We'd already been climbing for fifteen days. How much longer would it take? It seemed like we weren't making much progress. This route was new to me, and even on a familiar one, conditions are so variable that we can never predict exact schedules.

The next day I made a carry to Camp 3 with a couple of Sherpas. We stopped for a snack at Camp 3 and then fixed another 1,000 feet of rope toward Camp 4. I remember again looking up to the summit of Everest. It looked so far away. Then I looked back down at Camp 2, where just yesterday, Camp 3 had looked so far away. I realized we really were making progress.

Reflections

Planning a steady climb. The purpose of climbing each day was to establish a safe path up the mountain. The path is knowledge and experience. If we didn't establish our route, each day would be as hard and as difficult as the day before. Sometimes people spend most of the day discovering new problems and dealing with obstacles at random, rather than establishing the path that will make it possible to get over the obstacles the next day.

On this expedition, we had a clear logistical plan. We knew when we were going to move supplies, and what we were going to move. Each team member had clear responsibilities that meshed with those of the others. This removed a lot of potential stress.

Taking stock of accomplishments. It's important sometimes to pause, look back, and recognize how far we've come. Sometimes we can become overwhelmed by the big picture. Halfway through the project, all we can see is how far we still have to go. When we look back, though, we can be proud of what we have achieved.

Taking time out. Another way of relieving the pressure of a long, hard endeavor is to take time out. On Everest we could not go full tilt all the time. About once every three days, each climber would rest, either at base camp or Camp 2. We had to take rest days or risk becoming so exhausted our bodies would just stop.

Have you ever been so close to your summit that you could see it, almost grasp it, but you did not have the mental or physical energy to continue? You may say, "I'm just going to work as hard as I can for as long as I can, and just maybe I won't collapse until I get this job done." Sometimes when you get close to your goal, you push yourself even harder and become exhausted, so that you are no longer physically or mentally capable of climbing your mountain. You burned out—you forgot to take the time to recharge. When we take breaks from our work, we can rebuild physically and mentally.

Willi Unsoeld once wrote, "You go to nature for an experience of the sacred. You go there to re-establish your contact with the core of things, in order to come back into the world of man and operate more effectively."

What do you do to refresh yourself and give yourself time to regain strength for the next effort? Where do you go to re-establish contact with the core of things?

20

Holding Firm

Once we got onto the mountain, the climbing teams changed almost daily. I climbed with Steve and Geoff some days, and on others with Jim or Johnny. Still, there were a few climbers with whom I rarely worked. I climbed with Don only once, and never with Jean, Peggy, Dave, or Diana. I barely saw Dave and Diana. The two of them seemed to be on an entirely different circuit—when I was at one camp, they were at the one just above me, or just below. But none of the separations was deliberate. Personal preferences aside, the team never allowed itself to grow cliquish or factionalized. If anyone had reservations about anyone else, they were kept private.

As the days passed, we continued poking our route higher on the mountain. Up to Camp 3, then higher, up toward Camp 4, set up on the shoulder between Everest and Lhotse, that ridge of snow called the South Col. The weather was sweet and clear, and the team went higher, working together in even-tempered concert. Getting higher, getting closer!

Unlike last year's expedition team, we had a rock-solid understanding we had agreed to back in Seattle, before we hopped on the airplane and left U.S. airspace. There would be no spontaneous summit bids for us. Jim and Don, our leaders, wouldn't even choose the first summit team until the group had set the entire route and established Camp 4, the high camp on the South Col. Once that happened, the three climbers who had climbed highest on the mountain while staying strong and healthy would be offered the first shot at the summit. Then, while the other climbers put the finishing touches on the route, the first team would retreat to base camp for a few days of rest, gathering strength at the lower altitude before setting out for the final sprint to the summit.

I'm sure everyone felt a few rumbles. It's inevitable, when personal goals compete with group needs. But the infrastructure stayed together. We had a team and a plan, and the teammates were committed to furthering the prospects of both, even when opportunity or misfortune tempted them to do otherwise.

For instance, at one point late in the route-setting process, Johnny was carrying an early-morning load up near the top of the South Col, just 3,000 feet from the summit. It was a beautifully calm morning, but our first summit team was still resting at base camp, so Johnny and the others were playing support climbers, just stocking the camps. Seeing Johnny carrying a load within striking distance of the mountaintop, a summit-bound Frenchman was perplexed. "You better get to the summit while you have the chance," he said.

Johnny shook his head. "Nah. Not my turn."

The Frenchman rolled his eyes and gestured heavenward. "It is insane," he said, "to have these skies and just sit beneath them."

Johnny shrugged and continued up with his load. He'd take his shot when it came to him.

Charlie Shertz wasn't even going to get a shot—this much became clear during his first journey above Camp 1. Despite Charlie's years of high-altitude climbing, this time his body was not cooperating in the thin atmosphere. Noticeably weakened at Camp 1, Charlie pushed himself up to Camp 2 the next morning, but at

21,500 feet and only two days above the ice fall, he succumbed to the nausea and severe headache of altitude sickness. He couldn't eat. He knew his climb on Everest was over.

He retreated to base camp that afternoon, and he easily could have continued back to Kathmandu, back to the world of hot showers and fresh food, and then home. But Charlie was dedicated to our expedition and committed to seeing it succeed. He stayed at base camp, helping Bob Singer and Larry MacBean work the logistics until the entire group finished climbing, dismantled the route, and left for Kathmandu.

Even when the bonds were holding tight, though, I could feel the intimations of personal ambition. Who was the highest on the route? When am I going to catch up?

Reflections

Be patient and adjust. On Everest it was critical that we adjust to each elevation change, both physiologically and psychologically. Charlie was excited finally to be climbing on the mountain. When he arrived at Camp I, he mentioned feeling a little nauseated. After a restless night, he woke up even more nauseated, with a headache, and he couldn't eat. Instead of turning around and heading back to base camp or spending another day acclimating to the elevation of Camp 1, Charlie made the decision to continue up another 2,000 feet. At Camp 2 he felt far worse. The climb was probably over for Charlie only because of his impatience: he did not take the necessary time to adjust to the new plateaus.

Some people are climbing the ladder of success so quickly they don't take the time to reflect and integrate what they have learned on the lower rungs. It is imperative that we be patient and adjust to plateaus of change and growth before moving forward. If we don't build our foundation of strength, values, and competence, we may find ourselves at an altitude we can't cope with.

Make a commitment. Our ability to make commitments is influenced by our past experiences. It took three months for me to commit psychologically to the second Everest expedition because I was afraid that this climb might turn out like the previous one. When I was first invited, I was not there emotionally, only physically. I was not really contributing; I was holding back, not taking full responsibility. Until we commit there is always hesitancy and resistance.

Once I confirmed my commitment, about a month before we left the States, it was as if a thousand-pound weight had been lifted from my shoulders. I began taking an active part in team decisions; I began to get to know the other team members. The more I contributed and took part, the more the other team members accepted me.

Three things helped me commit. Knowing I had to be part of this team to reach my personal goal. Knowing the team needed me. And becoming clear on the reasons I wanted to climb the mountain.

What past experiences are you holding onto that may be preventing you from committing yourself fully?

Stay committed in adversity. Charlie regrouped after his setback. He could easily have gone to base camp and left for home, but his dedication and commitment to the team was stronger. If Charlie had left, it would have been detrimental to our team morale. Because he stayed, he modeled commitment and helped strengthen the bonds of our team.

Johnny was not going to be coaxed into ditching the team to achieve his own personal success. His commitment to the team and its overall success was more important. Sometimes we have to put group needs ahead of our own even when our needs are not being met.

Commitment is a choice we all make in our daily lives, in our personal relationships and our business relationships. Today fewer people are deeply committed to their companies. Mergers, downsizing, restructuring, administrative upheavals—they don't encourage loyalty. But even if company loyalty is low, people often remain committed to their fellow workers and clients with whom they have forged personal bonds. A good team can get a company through its avalanches.

21

A Leader's Decision

In the end, the daily assignments were Jim's decisions. He was the leader, the final authority. Alone or in consultation with co-leader Don, Jim made what we considered fair decisions, and he stuck by them. And for a while, that was fine.

Jim was doing a good job; he was doing right by me, as far as I could tell. I liked climbing with him—when we were on the same rope, I knew I could trust him with my life. But the pressure of leadership separated Jim from the rest of the team. As the expedition went on and the tension on the team increased, the pressure would force him to make some decisions that would cause dissension.

There were many advantages to getting tapped for the first summit team. It's the peak of the expedition: everyone is still focused on the climb, and there's virtually no risk of running out of supplies. When you're on Everest in the fall, climbing earlier means having a better shot at avoiding a winter storm. And if something goes wrong in mid-attempt—a storm, an accident, or illness—there's more time to retreat, wait while the others make their attempts, then try again.

We all wanted to go first.

I was on my third carry to Camp 3 with Steve and Jim. This time we planned to spend the night at the higher camp, then set out early the next morning to fix the rest of the line up to the South Col at 26,200 feet, where we'd establish Camp 4. But then, just as the three of us crawled into our sleeping bags at Camp 3 that afternoon, the horizon turned dark. Through the door of the tent we could see a black line of clouds sweeping across the pale blue sky, closing straight for us.

"I hate to be the voice of doom," Steve said, peering out toward the oncoming storm, "but it doesn't look good."

I nodded. "I think we better get out of here."

Jim didn't argue. An exposed camp on the Lhotse Face was the last place you wanted to ride out a heavy blizzard, with all that extra weight increasing the snowpack and the danger of avalanche. We rolled out of bed, threw on our down suits and boots, and plodded down the steep, icy slope back to Camp 2.

The snowstorm hit at dusk, and by the next morning a thick layer of clouds had seized onto the entire mountain. We couldn't move in either direction. We spent the next day huddled with the other climbers at Camp 2, hiding in our sleeping bags while the winds tore across the mountainside. But even when the climb itself cannot proceed, the business of the climb goes on. So as the storm raged that afternoon, and as the murky light faded to dusk, Jim and Don sat down to talk strategy.

So far the weather had been good to us. We had been moving quickly, and now, after two weeks, we were close to finishing the route. If the winter winds and snow kept their distance, we were in excellent position to send everyone who wanted to go up to the summit. But counting on another ten days of perfect weather — well, that was one monumental "if."

Time was the bottom line. No matter how smoothly things had gone, we were moving into the end of September now. The days were sliding away, and already we were pinned down by a massive storm. If we kept to our original plan — the one we'd all agreed on in Seattle, the one that held us all together — and didn't choose the first summit team until we had finished the route, we'd keep everyone on the mountain for a least another four or five days. Counting the three days of rest a summit team would require at base camp after that, following the original plan would push the series of summit attempts into October. And on Everest, October is frequently a wild, wintry month of snowstorms and windstorms.

Suddenly it seemed that we were getting behind the game. The other teams on the west side were sending their summit climbers down to rest at base camp. The French and Korean climbers were already getting ready to head for the summit. And here we were all up at Camp 2. So Jim and Don made a decision: forget the plan. We could no longer afford to wait until the entire route was set. Once it was calm enough to move, the first summit team would descend to base camp. The rest of the climbers would go up the mountain to finish off the route to the South Col and then build Camp 4.

Now all they needed to do was designate who was going to be on that first summit team.

Jim and Don had decided to stick with most of the original precepts of their plan, only with a slight variation. The three climbers who had climbed the highest on the route got to go first. Working on the route to Camp 4 had qualified Jim and me. Steve's afternoon at Camp 3 ushered him in. But Steve wasn't the only climber to have reached that high, and judging strength is always so subjective.

When word filtered through camp, the rumbling gathered force. Jim and Don had laid out four summit teams: Jim, Steve, and me on the first team; Don, Diana, and Dave on the second: Geoff and Johnny on the third team, and Peggy and Jean on the fourth. The news didn't bring unanimous joy. Geoff—working on his third attempt on the mountain—was frustrated to find himself so far down the list. Diana was furious that she was not included on the first summit team.

Reflections

Sharing information. Any leader who puts himself on the first summit team, no matter the circumstances, is bound to face criticism. As the rumbling became public on our team, Jim was no longer above reproach. Leaders are not guaranteed respect; it's earned, and one little mistake can erase it in a second. Everything Jim had done right up to that point was now questioned. It's like putting a drop of ink in a glass of water: it doesn't take long before the entire glass is tainted.

Also, Jim and Don made the decision. If it had been open for discussion by the entire team, even if not made by consensus, they probably would have been able to avoid such repercussions. Leaders must share information. The entire team must be involved if they are to buy into the plan. In the end, though, the responsibility for the decision is the leader's alone.

Adapting to circumstances. One of the hardest things a leader does is to take a long, hard look at a plan he or she has put in place, realize it's not working, and make the decision to change it. At this point in our climb, we were falling behind owing to unforeseeable conditions. We had to adapt. When our original strategy isn't working, we cannot afford to be so invested in it that we lose the flexibility we need to regroup and continue.

Can I lead? Five years after this, I decided to lead my own expedition to K2. It was a whole new challenge, a new world of responsibility, pressure, and expectations. Every successful climber has to approach a mountain with a dream, but when you lead an expedition you have to dream big enough for an entire group of people. More than that, you have to have the tenacity to turn that dream into reality. As an expedition leader, I'd have to decide on our route. I'd have to choose the team, give them a sense of mission, and motivate them. As on all expeditions, every climber would take responsibility for himself or herself. But responsibility for the team—the group's success, the lives of the climbers—would rest most heavily on my shoulders. Could I carry it? I wouldn't know until I took that first step, but I had the advantage of having watched other leaders and learning from their experiences.

22

Don't Worry

I was worried on Everest. We were at Camp 4, our high camp. Steve Ruoss and I shared a tent. We ate a quick dinner at four p.m., then set our alarms for nine that evening. To have daylight at the summit and during the descent back to camp, we'd need an early start. We would start climbing at midnight.

Steve dozed off immediately, but sleep was far from me. Even in my down sleeping bag, with two layers of polypropylene, the thin, frigid air sucked the heat from my body. The minutes crawled by, the hours stretched and sagged. Eventually the sun set and darkness came.

Time seemed to hang suspended. I could barely lie still, and Steve was unconscious! How could I be here wide awake while Steve was sleeping as if nothing in the world could bother him? How dare he sleep while I was lying awake worrying? Have you ever been wide awake at night with the "thinkies," as Scott Fischer used to call them, while your partner or spouse slept? Did you ever want to nudge him, just a little—c'mon, just a little?—so he would be awake and as miserable as you? That's how I felt! I wanted to shake Steve awake.

His chest moved with deep, clear breaths. I checked my own breathing. Also okay. No headache, no nausea. I was fine. But how would I be tomorrow, on the summit day? I'd kept up with Jim and Steve so far, but tomorrow was the crucial moment. New territory. More steep faces, more cliffs, gullies filled with deep, soft snow. Knee-deep for Jim and Steve was a long way up my thigh.

And on it went—worry worry worry. Each thought escalated out of proportion. building to a crescendo, all the worst things that could happen. No wonder I couldn't sleep!

Reflections

How can you not worry? I admit it, I'm a worrier. I'm working on it, though, and truthfully this is one of the hardest things for me to change. I worry about things like how I'm going to handle my two sons going off to climb some big mountain (right now they're all of three and four years old). I worry about my career. I worry about money. I just plain worry.

Worry affects our circulation, heart, glands, and nervous system. It causes fatigue and stress. Worry is an aspect of fear, and when we can learn to move through fear, we will have more energy.

When we worry about the future, often we get horribly worked up, and then after the fact, we look back and say "That wasn't so bad!" Our imagination is usually a lot worse than the actual event. Winston Churchill wrote, "When I look back on the worries, I remember the story of the old man who said on his deathbed that he had a lot of trouble in his life, most of which never happened."

Working out of worry. We can make our worry work for us if we turn worry into preparation and planning for the future. We do have control over preparing ourselves and our plans. We have control over our thoughts, and worry is a thought process. It takes practice to turn worry into productive action.

Sometimes our uncertainty about doing things we have never done before causes us tremendous trepidation. We begin to think about the all the things that can go wrong, and we're sure they will. And then, when we actually take action, we find ourselves saying it wasn't so bad. When we are afraid, our perception of reality can be very skewed.

The next time you begin to worry about the future, get a pencil and paper and write down your worry. Ask yourself, "Do I have control over this situation? What parts do I have control over and what don't I have control over?" Focus on what you can control, and then do something about it. What you can't control, let go. We'll never be able to control other people, either their thoughts or their actions. Once you understand this, it frees you to focus on your own thoughts and actions.

Here is a checklist that helps me:
1. Stop and project: How would I react if something went wrong? Take control of your thoughts to stay sane.
2. Accept it: I am human. What is this negative stress doing to me?
3. Make a list: What I'm worried about, both big and small.
4. Separate the list: What can I control, and what can't I control?
5. Stop for analysis: Have I listed everything?
6. Dismiss the things I can't control: Tear them up, don't waste time and energy on them.
7. Take action: Reorganize and prioritize the things I can control. Keep a list and cross things off as I accomplish them; it feels good to cross things off.

Worrying about the past does us absolutely no good either. The past is gone; it won't happen again. Learn from your past, apply those lessons to the present or future, and then let it go.

23

The Lottery

It was past midnight now, and Steve had finished dressing. For a moment he sat by the door, watching me adjust my socks and pull on my boots. I'd heard the Sherpas gathering outside our tent a few minutes earlier, crunching in the ice and chattering to themselves. Jim was already outside, adjusting his crampons, slinging on his backpack.

They wouldn't wait long, standing in the cold and wind. We were still a team, but today was different. You look after each other on summit day, but you think about yourself more.

I fumbled to strap on my crampons, and Steve glanced out the tent door. He shifted impatiently. "I'm going out," he said, and ducked through the flap. Panic shot through my stomach. I didn't want him to leave without me. Why am I so slow in the morning? I finished attaching my crampons and dashed out after him.

By the time I managed to get my pack on, Steve, Jim, and the Sherpas had already started away from camp. I hurried to adjust my oxygen mask, checking the regulator and setting the gauge. The empty tents rattled in the breeze as I started up across the snowfield, racing to catch my partners before they vanished into the darkness.

The snow was smooth and bone white, reflecting the light of a huge full moon. Stars scattered across the rest of the sky, and we walked without headlamps, our path lit by the pale glow from outer space. Enveloped in billowy down climbing suits, faces covered with heavy oxygen masks, we scuttled through a surreal landscape. Balanced between the sheer white light and deep black shadows, we were tiny and insignificant.

We moved as quickly as we could, kicking steps into the frozen crust on the snow. Climbing a few feet apart, we kept our heads down, concentrating on our own breathing and the rhythm of our steps. Even in a team of climbers, climbing becomes a solitary pursuit—especially in the outer fringe of the atmosphere, where communicating means shouting above your oxygen mask. It's hard enough to draw the breath to keep moving. Conversations are cut to the quick, thoughts and directions boiled down to hand signals and two-word fragments.

We climbed through the night. Up there, the altitude weighed heavily on every step. My heart hammered against my ribs, and the entire core of my body burned with the effort to breathe. Even with the hissing stream of pure oxygen, my lungs ached and my toes were numb with cold.

It hurt to move, but I ignored the pain. I focused on the task and kept moving, step after step. The rustle of my climbing suit, the squeak of the crampons in the dry snow. No dark thoughts, just effort. Occasionally I'd stop for a breather: a few deep pulls of oxygen and a bit of leg swinging. Then we'd start up again, and I'd return my attention to my feet, counting steps. At one hundred, I'd take ten seconds to catch my breath. At two hundred, I'd reach a hand up to crack my oxygen mask, breaking the film of ice formed by my moist exhalation.

Appa and Pemba had dropped back and were far below us. We were making good time and gaining altitude quickly. Around five a.m. we rested for a moment. Jim craned his neck to look down for Appa and Pemba. Steve and I shared some water with Pasang while Jim squinted, searching for them in the faint morning light. After a moment, a hiss broke the heavy breaths clouding his mask: "Shit!"

We all looked at Jim, still gazing down the mountainside. His voice was small and muffled in his mask. "They turned around!"

My jaw dropped. Steve looked over at me, lowering the water bottle from his mouth. "Well," he said. I followed Jim's gaze and stared down numbly at the figures retreating in the distance.

We were hundreds of feet away, and the two Sherpas—along with two of our oxygen tanks—were retreating. That was the oxygen we estimated that we needed to get to the summit and back. For a moment we stood there, mute, helpless, watching them vanish into the blackness.

"What happened?" Jim murmured. Sick or injured men would move slowly, but even at a distance we could see they were making good time as they plodded down the path, retracing the steps we'd made hours earlier. So what was it? Fatigue? Fear? A collapse of the will? It didn't matter now.

I pictured the mountain, trying to calculate how long we'd been climbing and how close we were to the summit. Could we make it there and back to camp with one bottle of oxygen apiece? Time to make a decision. We figured each tank had about six hours left. Since Appa and Pemba had vanished, we had only one replacement for the four of us.

A gust of wind rushed past. I leaned on my ice ax; Steve shifted his weight. Budgeting at least three hours to cruise to the top and then back to our camp made the entire trip about two hours beyond our oxygen supply.

Maybe we could squeak by—maybe we could survive the trip without oxygen. It had been done before. But maybe we couldn't.

"That's it, then." Jim's voice was thin in his mask. "We go back down and try again tomorrow."

I gazed up toward the summit, then back down the ridge where we'd struggled for the past two hours. There had to be another way. After all this time and all this effort, we couldn't just turn around. The weather was perfect, and there was no way to guarantee that it would hold on for another twenty-four hours. We had to get at least one person up there.

Steve, Jim, Pasang, and I had reached the moment when that decision had to be made. Someone had to take the extra oxygen bottle and at least try. The question was, who would that person be? All I could think to say was, "Let's draw straws."

Steve nodded. "Right." Jim mulled it over, looked up at the ridge, then back at us. He shrugged. "Fine." Jim looked over at Pasang. "Choose a number between one and ten."

Now my heart was racing. I felt myself starting to float out of my boots and off the ridge. We were going to draw for it. Somehow, deep down inside, I knew beyond a shadow of a doubt that I was going to win—I was going to the summit. Alone. I dug in my crampons. Even though this was a very brief process, I prayed. Please dear God, let it be me. No! Don't let it be me. I wanted to go. So much of my life was focused on this, so many years had led to this moment. But just now the thought of being alone up there, without Jim, Steve and Pasang, left me terrified.

Pasang peered back at Jim. Choose a number? What sort of wacko Sahib game was this? But he did what he was asked. Pasang nodded back at Jim, who turned to Steve.

"Eight," Steve said.

They both looked at me.

"Four."

"I'll take six," Jim said. We all looked over at Pasang.

"Three," he said. "It's three."

The three of them looked at me. We'd already been standing for a few minutes. The cold was seeping through my boots, crawling up my toes and into my ankles. My fingers were numb. I could see the others shifting in their boots. We had to start moving.

Reflections

What is it worth to me? At that moment, I realized that in the end, every summit boils down to what you're willing to risk to pursue your passion and make your dreams come true. Jim, Steve, and Pasang could continue to the summit with me if they were willing to risk running out of oxygen. Steve and Jim decided that for them, the summit of Mount Everest was not worth the risk; they turned back and began their descent. Pasang, however, was willing to join me in the final leg of our journey: for him, the summit of Everest was worth the risk.

There's a climbers' saying, "There are no old bold mountaineers." When we're starting out, the adventurous spirit is the spark that ignites our endeavors. Then we accept the discipline that keeps us alive by limiting our risk level to what our competence can handle. The self-confidence we build creates a passion for greater achievement. But what happens at that point if we're not willing to accept more risk?

Striking out alone. It was not easy saying goodbye to Steve and Jim. Even though we weren't roped together, they were a psychological support for me. I would no longer reach the summit with the comfort and fellowship of my friends. In my climb to the top, I felt profoundly alone.

Sometimes all of us feel profoundly alone. It's precisely then that we must rely on our inner strength and courage to keep moving forward. The true test of self-confidence is what we do when there is no one left to turn to. Sometimes we have to walk away from everything that has meant security to us in order to reach our dreams. Some of us need to find ourselves in a drastic situation to discover the self-confidence deep within us, while others rely on it every day. The key is to find and use that inner strength. Have the courage to seek out and take that extra step. Have the courage to say goodbye.

Even though I had to finish my climb almost alone, it was a team effort. Up to Camp 4, all that work—ferrying supplies, setting the route—had been done by many people. But above Camp 4, we were on our own. A team can only take you so far; after that, it's up to you.

When you have made your climb in the best way possible, and one formidable step lies between you and your goal, are you determined enough to leave your security behind and take that step on your own initiative?

Windows of opportunity. I was lucky. But luck only goes so far in the mountains before it runs out. I was able to take advantage of my luck because I was prepared. Luck is what happens when opportunity and preparation meet.

Windows of opportunity present themselves for only a short period, and already we could see the window closing. How do you know whether it's really a once-in-a-lifetime opportunity? Often you can't know for sure until after the fact. But if it is, and you pass it up, you will certainly regret it. Steve and Jim never did reach the summit of Everest.

An Associated Press survey asked people over age fifty about the regrets in their lives. Fifty-nine percent of them said they did not regret the things they had done in their lives. Fifty-nine percent also said they had regrets about the things they hadn't done.

Ruth Simmons, president of Smith College, writes, "If you are the kind of person who listens to conservative advice, you may do okay in life, but you probably won't ever be a fantastic leader. You have to take risk, and you also have to go against conventional wisdom, because conventional wisdom doesn't make for startling advances in society."

24

Alone on the Peak

Even in the cold the sun's rays were palpable, as if they carried a physical weight down through the pale blue sky and pure air. I could see everything. Above, a few wispy clouds skimmed by the sun. Behind me I could look down into Nepal. All but a few of the tallest peaks were covered by thick, billowing clouds. The sky was clearer above the brown plains of Tibet, spread out before me.

The wind began to gust and blew my hat off. It hovered three feet away from me for a few moments, then fell eight thousand feet into Tibet.

I hesitated: should I go on? But the summit was like a magnet drawing me. When you can see it, the magnitude of the work you have done to get there overrides any thought of turning around.

Now I was only seventy-five feet away. Walking carefully, minding the crack in the ridge and the tip of my ice ax, my crampons squeaking in and out of the snow. One foot in front of the other.

Fifty feet. So close, but I wouldn't let myself feel it yet. Not until I was there. Something was swelling inside me, but I suppressed it. I had to keep moving, stay focused. Walking faster, feeling the adrenaline starting to flow, surging through my veins and running hot into my fingers and even my numb toes.

Twenty-five feet. The grateful triumph could no longer be forced down. Now I knew I was going to make it.

Ten feet. This was it. It was so strange. After everything, I was walking onto the summit of Mount Everest. It was right there, I could see it clearly just ahead of me. The last few steps, just a little higher, and then there was nothing. The end of the ridge, and then nothing but the clear, empty air.

I stopped climbing. There was nowhere else to climb.

I was standing on top of the world.

I felt it now, everything I'd kept bottled up as I came up the ridge. It billowed up from my core, a blinding wave of emotion. I could finally let go of the months of controlling my thoughts and channeling all my energy toward this one purpose. Behind my glasses my eyes blurred. I was wide open now, and I was aware of everything. The wind in my hair, the sweat on my back, the blood washing through my wrists and ankles. I made it. For myself, for Steve and Jim, for everyone.

Pasang was still ten minutes away. So it was just me. A small patch of snow, the vast sky, and me. The cloud of emotion thinned and vanished. My eyes were dry again. Now I felt strange.

I was on top of the world, but I was alone. This wasn't how I wanted it to happen. During all those years of wishing for it, dreaming about it, and working on it, I never once imagined I'd be alone when I got to the summit. I wanted to hug someone, to make this dream explode into life by seeing it reflected in someone else's eyes. But I was on top of Everest by myself.

Reflections

Are you prepared to reach your goals alone? Realizing that you may be alone at your moment of greatest accomplishment emphasizes the importance of believing in yourself and what you do. You need to be certain of your reasons for seeking a goal, because you may be the only one who will understand it. It takes courage to set lofty goals for ourselves; it takes courage to believe in ourselves and believe we truly deserve greatness.

Have you ever gone home and tried to share an accomplishment with your spouse or partner, only to find out he or she doesn't understand why you did it, or why you're so proud of having succeeded? Having supportive people around us is important, but we can't depend on others to validate our lives. If we are true in our commitment to our personal vision, we will find the validation we need within ourselves.

25

Down to Earth
on Top of the World

Then Pasang came up. He pumped his ice ax in the air, hooting and yipping with everything he had left in his lungs. The sight popped the lid off my emotions again, and I walked over to him, reaching out to give him a hug. "We did it," I said, my eyes going hot and cloudy again.

You might think that when people have just climbed the highest mountain in the world, they could just kick back and relax for a while. Not true. We brought thirty-five banners with the logos of our corporate sponsors to the top with us. We had to photograph those banners before we could go back down.

After doing our job, we snapped a few pictures of each other, and I shot a series of panoramas. Then I reached into my pocket for my own artifacts. Climbing the mountain gave me something to take away, so it felt only appropriate to leave a small part of me behind.

I had a little piece of turquoise a Tibetan yak herder had given me in 1987. He had lived in the shadow of the mountain for his entire life but never dreamed of climbing it, so I promised to take something of his to the top. I had a little bag of blessed rice from our altar at base camp the day we set out for the summit. I had a prayer scarf, a snapshot of me with David, and a Susan B. Anthony silver dollar.

I looked at my watch. It was getting late now, after eleven. We didn't have that much time, but I still felt I had to ground myself. I thought about the mountain's spirit: the Mother Goddess of the Earth. I thanked her for being kind enough to let me climb her. And I prayed she'd let me get down in one piece, too.

I looked at my watch again. We'd already been on the summit for about forty-five minutes. I caught Pasang's eye and gestured down. He looked surprised.

"Now?"

"Soon. In a minute." I said.

We stood together, looking out over the world beneath us. I wanted to remember everything. The cold, dry air between my lips, the wind pushing against my back, the way the silvery wisps of cloud jetted across the sky. I needed to remember it, to keep the image deep inside the vaults in my memory bank. This was the top of Everest. The dream of a lifetime.

I looked around for some perfect image that would objectify why I'd come, now and forever. But nothing came into focus. It was hard to believe, after so many years, but the summit of Everest was just snow and ice. A mountain summit, pretty much like any other mountain summit.

I was contemplating this when Pasang said, "We spend two months getting to the mountain, carrying things up the mountain, climbing the mountain. We work like dogs, then spend so little time on top and now we go back down. What's the meaning?"

I just shook my head.

Reflections

You can't stop here. When you get to the top, you've only done fifty percent of the work. You have to get back down. Some people—and organizations—spend all their energy, resources, and vision getting to the top, but the top is the most vulnerable place to be. We cannot survive on top of our mountains.

Resting on our laurels is dangerous. You know what I mean: "I'm good at my job; all I have to do is come to work, perform, and go home." This is a false sense of security, especially in today's competitive, fast-changing world. After you reach the top it is more important than ever to look for and create opportunities to learn, grow, and improve—so that you can climb new mountains. Are you still challenged by what you do, or are you sitting on top of your mountain with nowhere to go? People who live on yesterday's accomplishments deny themselves tomorrow's adventures.

When you have achieved success, you can't kick back and relax. You will have more decisions to make. Staying centered and focused may be more difficult than it was when you had a single goal ahead of you. With all its joys and opportunities, success still demands the same level of maturity that you brought to striving for it.

What did it all mean? After forty-five minutes on the summit of Everest, Pasang and I independently had the same thought: Is this what we worked for months, or even years, to achieve? Nonetheless, both of us were to return to climbing great mountains. A renewal of vision, energy, and resources is necessary to get back down and start again.

Most people expend most of their life's energy working. And in the end, what does it mean? It's difficult to justify our efforts unless they are based in vision and passion. Are you following your passion?

Leaving your mark. As humans have done for millennia, I left a mark at the site of my achievement. The objects I placed on the summit symbolized my social and spiritual values. One was the image of the person dearest to me, my husband, and another was a token from someone I barely knew: I am bound in some way to humans everywhere. These were objects representing my respect for the spirituality of the place, and a symbol of my respect for strong women.

Now that I am a professional speaker, I have an opportunity to leave a different kind of mark on others. We all leave behind something in this life. What kind of mark do you want to leave on the world?

26

The Climb's Not Over

Peggy Luce and Geoff Tabin, along with three Sherpas, summitted Everest just three days after Pasang and me.

The weather turned dark the day Peggy and Geoff got back to Camp 2. Conditions grew more violent the next morning, and with no end to the storm in sight, everyone except Steve retreated to base camp.

We were heading into mid-October now, dangerously close to the point where the winds would blow the weather window shut for the year. We waited for an entire week while the mountain winds roared without pause. Up at Camp 2, Steve spent his days working to shore up the tents. Base camp was untouched by the gales; we sat in a warm autumn sun, in T-shirts and shorts, hearing the constant deep roar of the mountain like a jet aircraft in the sky.

As the days passed, tension built. Earlier we had all been joined by a single ambition, a goal we knew each of us could reach with the help of the others. But once some team members had reached that goal, agendas and allegiances started to shift.

The team divided into two groups: the ones who were still hoping to summit, and Geoff, Peggy, and I, the ones who had. Charlie had given up early and shifted to a supporting role. Jean, though, wore his disappointment like a mourning cloak; he kept his eyes downcast and rarely spoke at meals.

My perspective was changing, too. While I was still climbing, I found it hard to think about anything but the mountain. I blocked out anything else—David, my family, what I might want to do with my life when I got home. But once I stood on top, then came down and walked out of the ice fall for the last time, I could feel something inside me turning homeward.

Steve, Johnny, Diana, Dave, Don, and Jim had a very different outlook: the summit. Officially, we were still committed to getting as many climbers to the top as possible. But what was possible? Winter was nearing and soon the blizzards would be on us. We had to set up a departure schedule. Jim brought up the subject in the dining tent at lunch one day.

He began by describing the realities of autumn in Nepal. If we waited too long, the jet stream could stop us from salvaging our gear from the high camps. And one big storm could dump enough snow onto the moraine to make it impossible for yaks and porters to help us. If that happened, we'd have to leave behind thousands of dollars' worth of equipment. "We're taking a big risk," he concluded. "If we don't start thinking about leaving, we might not get out."

Diana's face was stormy, her eyes desperate. She'd worked so hard on this expedition, she'd spent so long dreaming about it, she'd invested so much of herself. "I don't want to be rushed," she said. "Just because other people have made the summit doesn't mean we shouldn't get our fair shot."

Don weighed in firmly: "No matter what happens, we've got to have a definite end date. Otherwise we'll never get out of here."

Our permit kept us legal through November 3, but even if the winds lifted for a few days, they wouldn't stay away for an entire week, let alone two or three. Don suggested setting the deadline on October 20. That gave the climbers almost two weeks to make the summit, and the rest of us a date to plan our departure.

When the wind ebbed enough on October 10, Johnny climbed up to meet Steve at Camp 2. They would be the next summit team, ascending the Lhotse Face for the South Col whenever the weather allowed them to risk it. Diana, Dave, and Don would follow for the final attempt on the summit. It was a tight schedule, especially at the tail end of the climbing season, but with a little luck, we might pull it off.

Reflections

Commitment to the team. Even though I myself had reached the summit, the climb wasn't over. I still had a responsibility and commitment to the team to help as many climbers as possible reach to the top. I was aware that internally I was already heading home, but I made a conscious effort to do everything I could to remain positive and encourage others to stay motivated.

When your climb's over, how do you respond to your teammates?

Closure. In any endeavor, there has to be closure. For those who hadn't reached the summit, the lack of closure burdened them with dissatisfaction and wore them out mentally. Jim took the first step in curing this malaise by stating that it was time to establish an end date and letting everyone supply some input. The fact that everyone was heard clarified the issue and helped us all to accept the group's decision, even if it disappointed some of us.

Before we had our discussion, we had no end date. Our motivation was low and getting lower by the day. Once we set a date, though, morale picked up. Once again we could focus on getting back up the mountain, instead of watching commitment drain away toward home.

27

Values

Steve and Johnny were back on the mountain, climbing toward Camp 3 on their summit attempt. About two thousand feet above them, just setting out from Camp 3, Steve could see a team of Spanish climbers heading for the South Col, small colored specks against the sheer white face. Steve kept climbing, moving quickly up the fixed line, looking up occasionally to track the Spanish team's progress. In eighteen hours they could be starting out for the summit. Steve glanced up again, and something else caught his eye.

It was moving: another speck, only this one was coming down the face—rocketing down, out of control, spinning on the windblown snow, bouncing off ridges, flying, then landing hard and cartwheeling for a few dozen yards.

Steve turned and gestured to Johnny. He had already seen it. They turned and watched together. They knew it was a body. It fell like a comet past them, then came to a stop. Steve and Johnny made the decision to turn back and investigate.

When he leaned over the body, Steve knew the Sherpa climber had been dead for at least twelve hours. He was frozen solid. Someone, it seemed, must have thrown him down on purpose. Steve looked up at the Lhotse Face. Next to him, his Sherpa companions were crossing and uncrossing their arms, their faces gloomy and clouded. No one, they knew, would ever throw a white climber's body down the Lhotse Face.

Stunned, unsure what to do, Steve, Johnny, and the two Sherpas moved the body from where it had fallen to a more sheltered spot on the glacier. As it turned out, the French team had lost two Sherpas, and the French leader, on finding them, decided to hurl the bodies down the face. We never understood why.

It was now too late to move up to Camp 3, so Steve, Johnny, and the Sherpas retreated to Camp 2. At the next dawn, they were headed again to Camp 3.

The Spanish climbers' troubles had started the day before, when Sergei Martinez came down with a sinus infection. The cold, dry air exacerbated it, but Martinez felt well enough to keep going, so the party continued up to the col and then, early the next morning, toward the summit. The Spaniards climbed through the morning, making steady progress until they reached the lower prominence south of the true summit. Then Martinez grew too weak to continue; he sat down to wait while his teammates made the final push to the top. The other three Spanish climbers and their two Sherpas scampered to the summit, then turned around to collect their sick friend. Finding Martinez in dramatically worse shape— barely conscious, almost blind, and apparently sinking into cerebral edema—the climbers made a stretcher out of climbing rope and started pulling him down the mountain. His survival depended on a rapid descent.

Meanwhile, Johnny and Steve were climbing above Camp 3, heading to the South Col, back on track again. The weather was perfect, and the summit only twenty-four hours away.

Then the Spanish team came into view. When they met, Martinez's hands and feet were frostbitten and he had full-blown cerebral edema, the swelling of the brain tissues that is the most terrible manifestation of altitude sickness. Seeing how close to death he was, Steve and his companions turned around immediately and helped pull him down to Camp 2. Once again, they gave up their summit attempt.

By this point, Steve and Johnny were too exhausted to make another ascent. Diana, Dave, and Don got up to Camp 4, but they were turned back by high winds. The expedition had to head for home.

Reflections

On a climb, our core values are tested daily. Very often a decision must be made not just on technical grounds but on the basis of our character and ethics. Even though Steve and Johnny knew the falling man was dead, they had an ethical imperative to investigate and to take the time to show what respect they could in this extreme situation.

The Spanish climbers abandoned a severely ill member of their party so they could achieve their goal. This increased his danger, and theirs as they had to carry him down the mountain. I shouldn't rush to judgment on them, though: he may have concealed the gravity of his condition, much as Fredo had done on Pik Kommunizma; or the cultural expectations of his team may have been different from ours.

Values must be congruent with actions. Sometimes in life we become so focused on reaching our goals that we compromise our values. "The end justifies the means" is a saying so well known that few people remember where it originated. It is well to remember that it was a principle of Marxist-Leninist thought—and we know where that got the people who espoused it. If you make it your business to achieve your goal at any cost, the cost may include your values and self-respect.

This was one of the lessons I had learned on my first trip to Everest. In my haste to get to the top, I found myself compromising my values by not cooperating. I lost some respect for myself as a result.

The task of maintaining respect for values is up to each individual, but the leader of a team effort has a special responsibility in this regard. No one leads effectively without a rock-solid foundation provided by values. Other members are always scrutinizing the leader, analyzing whether he or she is acting consistently, quick to catch any wavering or hypocrisy. We're often reminded that consistent commitment to clear values is necessary for a parent raising children; it is also imperative in a leader of adults.

Values provide us with our foundation, the essence of who we are, and commitment gives us the strength and courage to take action.

It's good to remember, though, that we aren't born with a set of values. We learn them from our culture at large, and many kinds of experiences can modify them. Their outward expression may be affected by our opinions and culture. It's remaining true that counts, in the final analysis.

Values don't change, but the way we weight our values may alter over the years. For example, before I was a parent, I was willing to take major risks to climb mountains. My basic responsibility was to myself. Now, I am not willing to risk it all: my children need me.

What are your values now? How have they changed over the years and experiences you have had?

28

A New Vision

David and I are now parents of two young boys. When we made the decision to have children, David wanted me to promise him that I would not climb mountains any more. He said, "I don't want to be a single parent, and I want my children to know their mother."

We went around and around for months, getting nowhere. Finally I said, "I can't promise you I won't climb big mountains, but I will promise you I will be the best mother possible."

I do not climb big, dangerous mountains anymore. When we had our children, I realized that this was the most serious responsibility I'd ever undertaken. For thirty-six years, I had done exactly what I wanted to do. Now, though, it's not about me any more: it's about my children. It's my goal to encourage them to become confident, capable, caring people. We have new adventures every day. I do miss climbing, but I don't have any regrets.

The wonderful thing about life is that we change. We were meant to change. I have some new values now; I have a different vision of myself and where I'm heading.

I know some climbers who have children and continue to climb big mountains, staying away from their families for several months at a time. I also had friends who have died climbing, leaving families behind. At some point, we need to ask ourselves, "Why did I have children? What is most important here—my child, or me?"

As a parent and a professional, my biggest challenge is balance. What I've learned is that I have to remain true to my own values, not the values of other professional people. What works for others may not necessarily work for me. For example, I know I don't want to do a hundred presentations a year. I don't want to spend that much time away from my family. My values don't include sacrificing everything else in life to professional reputation and advancement, or to making money.

Just as I made decisions while climbing the mountain, we all must decide for ourselves what's important to us. And we must commit ourselves to live with those decisions. I've had the opportunity to be counseled by several very successful businessmen I've met while speaking. When I've told them about my children, they have given me some good advice: "Be careful how much time you spend away from your kids. My children are now grown, and I'm not real close to them."

One very successful speaker cautioned me with this story. "My grown daughter came to one of my seminars. Afterwards, many people came up to her and said 'You're father is incredible, you must be so inspired and proud!' When everyone had gone, she said, 'Dad, you may be a great seminar leader, but you were not a great dad.'" Those words struck a deep blow in his heart.

I don't want to be known as a great climber, or necessarily as a great speaker. I want to be known as a great mother first. And when I know I am a great mother, I can then focus my energies on excelling in my work.

Further Reflections

29

Support Systems

Who's on your support team? Of course we all have different support teams for the different aspects of our lives. One of the most important members of my team is my husband, David.

In 1993, I led a successful climb of K2, the second highest mountain in the world and one of the most difficult and dangerous to climb. Before I could fully embrace the climb I had to know what David thought about it. I was apprehensive about his answer, yet I couldn't really move forward without knowing I had his support. Awkwardly, I asked "So, what do you think about me leading a climb to K2?"

David just smiled: "Please, tell me more." He's always so calm.

"For the past several months I've been thinking about climbing K2. I just wanted to know what you think."

The discussion went on from there. Two hours later, David said, "If you need to go climb K2, I'll be here to support you."

It took the team two years to get permits and prepare for the climb. When we were on the mountain, I would open his letters, which trekkers brought periodically from Islamabad. There would be pieces of squashed dried fruit folded inside—probably to remind me of the great summer fruit harvest I was missing. He would send me flowers, dried and pressed. His words were always encouraging: "Dear Stacy, I know you're all doing well. I'm doing great back here. Have fun."

Imagine what would have happened if I'd received letters that said, "I'm worried sick about you. I can't sleep at night. I wish you were home." No one needs that kind of baggage. I didn't always have a strong supportive relationship, and I know what it's like not to have a supportive spouse. Life is tough enough without having someone undercutting you.

In order to climb these dangerous mountains, to focus one hundred percent on the task at hand, I had to have the support of David, and also of my other family members and friends. We all need strong support systems in our daily lives to help us achieve and be our best. Surround yourself with positive people who are there for you and want you to succeed. Elevate yourself with the help of others.

Of course, you are those other people's support system too. If you're setting out on an endeavor and depending on those back at home, it's important to set things right before you leave. Have you ever had an argument with your child, partner, or spouse before leaving for work? Where was your focus when you got to work? How much time and energy do we waste on the job when we're distracted by unresolved issues at home?

When we leave for a three-month climbing expedition, it's imperative that everything be set right at home before leaving. For me, it's a matter of life and death. In everyday life it's a matter of being effective at our work. The security of a stable support system makes us effective in managing our time, thinking clearly, and reducing our overall level of stress.

Being wise about the people among whom you choose to pursue your endeavors—on a mountain, in your career, and in the rest of your life—is part of planning.

30

Preparation

This is what I did to prepare myself for Mount Everest.

I began by gathering information on Everest, and specifically on the route we were attempting. I went to the library and read every book I could find on the subject. I went to slide shows; I talked to people who had attempted our route.

Once I knew a good deal about the route and the mountain, I could begin focusing on my specific goal. I used visualization. I mentally rehearsed being at base camp: what the surroundings looked like, how I felt, what I was doing. I visualized myself climbing the mountain; I visualized myself on the summit, and coming off the mountain safely. This mental rehearsal helped me to focus and organize myself.

I also drew on past experiences. All the mountains I had climbed were my training ground for Mount Everest. Each mountain presented some valuable challenges and learning experiences.

All personal preparation begins with mental preparation; otherwise, you have no vision. In these three steps—research, focusing, and drawing on experience—lies the mental preparation for climbing any mountain. It establishes belief in oneself and one's purpose. If I didn't believe in my self or my purpose, it would have been difficult to prepare emotionally and physically.

Emotional preparation involves both finding the support of other people, and putting one's own emotional life in order. I climbed Pik Kommunizma during my divorce from my first husband. I would find myself breaking down and crying right in the middle of climbing. I spent too much energy trying to be strong. I could not stay focused, and my unbalanced emotions left me physically and mentally drained.

Physical preparation builds stamina. It's more a lifestyle for me than a regimented training program. I am always active, and my activities complement one another. I run, ski, mountain bike, kayak, and climb as much as I can. I get enough sleep and eat a balanced diet.

The relationships among our mental, emotional, and physical states are quite interdependent. When you are not prepared in one of these aspects, it puts tremendous stress on the others. Not being physically prepared distresses one mentally and emotionally. On Pik Kommunizma, I wore out physically and mentally because I was emotionally overextended.

When I followed a balanced routine to prepare myself physically, mentally, and emotionally, it was easier for me to stay focused and committed to my goal of climbing Everest.

31

Self-Knowledge

People often say to me, "Oh, you are so courageous! It must take a lot of courage to climb." Yes, it takes immense courage to climb, but not for the reasons you may think.

One of the beauties of climbing is that it forces us to come face to face with ourselves. There are no facades. We don't have the luxury of hiding behind a lectern or a three-piece suit. We are stripped away, revealed—all our strengths and weakness, likes, dislikes, everything. The stress of climbing does not build character, it reveals it. Our real character is revealed for us to look at honestly, and then build upon.

When we first meet people, we often ask, "What do you do?" We are a culture that defines ourselves by our activities and accomplishments. For a long time I defined myself as Stacy Allison, the climber. Then it was Stacy Allison, first American woman to climb Mount Everest. That's an impressive title, but it's only a title. After having my children, I made the decision not to climb big mountains anymore. How do I define myself now?

When I didn't make it to the top of Everest on my first try, it was like losing my job, or even my identity. Another person may define her identity by her job: what happens when the company or agency falls apart? Then who is she? When a person is self-defined as the spouse of a successful or beautiful person, what happens when the marriage falls apart? Almost any unexpected loss can precipitate an identity crisis.

Some of us define ourselves through our appearance, avocations, or hobbies. The media encourage people to be "a beautiful woman," "a runner," or "a connoisseur." What happens when a person no longer has these qualities, physical capabilities, or interests? Then how do we define ourselves?

I have learned that who we are is what we are inside, not what we do. I define myself as a kind, caring, competitive risk-taker. What is most important to me are my children and husband. If I never climbed another mountain, I would still have the qualities that I think are most important within me.

32

Drowning in Fear

My husband and I enjoy whitewater kayaking. We also take our boats out in the ocean to surf them on the waves. I'm afraid of the ocean. There are big things that can eat you out there.

One day when we were surfing in the ocean, I was being somewhat timid and staying close to shore. David finally convinced me to go out to the bigger waves. To calm me down, we went way out beyond the breaking waves. I remember thinking to myself, "This isn't so bad. As a matter of fact, that was quite easy!"

I let down my guard, enjoying myself. Then, all of a sudden, I looked behind me to see a sneaker wave—the occasional extra-high wave that hits the Pacific coastline—coming right at us. Oh my, this is it, I'm going to drown.

Instead of paddling toward the wave or preparing to surf it, I froze. It crashed over me, flipping me upside down. Instead of rolling my kayak back up, I panicked. I came out of my boat, now even more vulnerable to those big things that can eat you. In fear, I grabbed hold of my kayak. Meanwhile, David was yelling to me,

"Let go of your kayak! If the waves catch it, it'll flip and hit you! Get away from your kayak!"

Okay. So I was trying to swim in to shore, and David was right beside me. I cried out to him, "David, help me, help! I can't swim in this! Help me!"

And he was yelling, "Stacy, stand up!"

"I can't! I can't!"

"Stacy, stand up!"

Finally the light went on. Oh, stand up. I stood up, and the water was only thigh-high.

Have you ever felt the helplessness of drowning in your fears? Fear distorts our perception of reality. When we're afraid, we lose our ability to think straight, and our decision-making processes are impaired.

One of the things I have to point out to people who read or hear about my climbing adventures is that courage isn't about conquering fear. The fear doesn't die; it doesn't disappear and never come back to life. Most of us have certain fears that we will never overcome. Instead, we learn to live with them. We can sweep fear under the carpet so we can't see it, but it's always there, waiting for the perfect opportunity to emerge—usually at the most inopportune times for us.

As a climber, as a kayaker, and as a professional speaker, I have learned to work with my fear and not let it wrap its tentacles around my legs and pull me under. Fear is just an appearance, not necessarily the reality of the situation. Sometimes we must look beyond appearance and emotion to see the truth about ourselves and the situation.

The first thing to remember is that it is all right to be afraid. Fear is nature's way of protecting us against destroying ourselves by acting rashly. But just because you're justifiably afraid at times, you don't have to become a fearful person. Realize that fear is an instrument of your survival; it is within you, like your strength or your intelligence. It is not an external force that is bigger than you.

Once you have understood the risk inherent in the thing that is causing you to fear, and once you assess your competence to face that risk, the only way to get rid of the fear is by acting. Our fear increases when we simply ignore or postpone action.

There are risks we should step away from, but when we simply run away from fear, it looms over us, getting larger and larger. When we move toward our fear, it becomes smaller.

Fear is our growing edge. It is not only the impetus to grow, but the bridge to it as well. You must go through it to experience the power of overcoming it. Until you summon the courage to move through it, rather than around it, you will not experience the higher awareness and fulfillment that lies on the other side. For many people, a sense of purpose compels them to make that first step; it overrides their pain and fear.

And finally, one powerful weapon against fear is humor. I was so sure I was drowning, but when I stood up in shallow water and realized how ridiculous I looked, I burst out laughing. My fear had paralyzed me, and my sense of humor set me free. It was amazing how the mood shifted and I could see I was safe!

33

Equipment

New mountaineering equipment comes out all the time, and people spend plenty on it, but it is still physical and mental factors that make or break a climb. The lighter, stronger gear has made it possible for many more people to climb, just because it's not as uncomfortable as it used to be. It's disquieting, though, to contemplate what may be a trade-off between convenience and security. People don't learn the skills they need for big mountains working out in a rock gym, and all the high technology in the world will never replace the long, hard process of learning.

People either make or break a climb. And people either make or break a business. It's quite common for a company to have an executive who thinks that upgrading the computer system or installing other high-tech wonders will turn around a failing enterprise or make a successful one far more productive. The usual first response is a chorus of groans from the staff. If the people who will use the technology aren't committed to mastering it and benefiting from it, their frustration will only undermine the enterprise and make a bad situation worse.

In James Golden's book *National Strategy in the Information Age,* the author comments that what will separate successful technology companies in the global market will be the people who stand behind the products, not the products themselves. The relationships people build are what create their customer loyalty.

If you are in a business that uses technology—and almost all do, these days—your competitors can easily buy or build the same equipment you use. But they can't hire your people (unless you are making them very unhappy). You may have state-of-the-art facilities and equipment and plenty of capital, but unless you can attract and retain skilled, creative, helpful people, you will have no competitive advantage.

Just as important as knowing what you need is knowing what you don't need. Climbers are sometimes fanatical about doing more with less; some of them even saw the handles off their toothbrushes to save weight. When we go higher up the mountain, we must make choices about what we leave out of our packs. The higher we go, the more difficult it is to carry loads owing to the lack of oxygen. For example, we carried books and games up to our second camp on the mountain, but up higher, we did not allow ourselves those luxuries. We took only those items necessary for our survival and success. At the highest levels, our tents are small and light; our food is freeze-dried. There are fewer supporting climbers: they are no longer needed. Everything is focused on efficiency in the rarefied, hostile environment.

34

The Right Mind-Set

On my second Everest expedition, I was again part of the team responsible for supplies. When we arrived in Kathmandu, we had the major chore of getting our 460 boxes of food and gear out of customs.

We Americans do not tend to be subtle. We burst through the doors into the customs agent's office and stated, "Here are our papers. We're here to get our boxes."

"Ahh, memsahib, these are not the correct papers. You'll have to come back tomorrow." That was fair.

The next day we met with the same fate. And then it was the weekend. By the next business day, we were steaming, to put it mildly. We were getting nowhere. We were here to climb a mountain, and we didn't have time for this process that we didn't even understand. The harder we pushed, the calmer the customs agent became.

At last it dawned on us. We had to sit down and drink tea with him. We had to build a relationship and get into the Nepalese mind-set. We had to pause. It took us eleven days of negotiations and a

$2,000 bribe to get our boxes out of customs. We learned what was important.

Isn't this what we must do in business to stay competitive and build relationships? We have to get into our customers' mind-set. Tony Alessandra calls this the "Platinum Rule." We all know the Golden Rule: Do unto others as you would have them do unto you. This doesn't work anymore, especially in the global marketplace. People and cultures are all different in their values, goals, and needs. We must treat our customers the way they want to be treated, not the way we want to be treated. This requires us to know about the people we are interacting with—what's important to them. We have to know what their needs are so that we can help them with their solutions.

This is just as true in personal life. My son Andrew, age three, was kicked out of preschool. My first reaction was, "I don't have time for this! I don't have time to look for child care, to look for a new school, I don't have time to have Andrew at home. I have a job." For a couple of weeks I was very resentful of his taking up my time. Then it dawned on me: I had to sit down and drink tea with him. I had to pause and listen to his needs—and I realized that he hadn't been ready for the demands of school; he needed to be at home for a while longer.

Are you undermining your endeavor by failing to pause, to drink tea, and build a relationship?

35

Looking beyond the Ordinary

I think my mother put it into words before I fully understood what climbing was to me. She knew exactly why I had to climb Mt. Everest when I made my decision. I remember she said to me, "Of course you should go. Climbing is how you express yourself."

And that's exactly what climbing is to me. That's why I was drawn to the sport, and why I continue devoting myself to it. Expression is what a painter does on canvas, what a writer can do with twenty-six letters in the alphabet. It's the key that unlocks my spirit, the clearest representation of who I am. When I am focused, climbing is almost an unconscious act for me. I don't have to drive myself; I'm already driven. Always higher, never bothering to look down, never worrying about what I might find above me. There may be difficulties ahead—of course there will be difficulties. Life is a constant maze of problems and puzzles.

Climbing has inspired me, shaped my life, and changed it. Climbing has given me confidence and strength. It has taught me how to be resourceful, how to challenge myself, and how to trust myself enough to take risks. I have learned to look beyond the ordinary and to transcend myself. Climbing stays with me when I'm building a house, making a speech, or interacting with my family.

Everest stays with me, too. The summit experience was ephemeral—it was gone in an hour. Now I have to think hard to remember what it felt like up there. But the climb itself is in the marrow of my bones, like all the other climbs and adventures and experiences in my life. It's in the friends I made while I was there. It's in what I learned about myself when I failed on my first attempt, and what I proved to myself when I dusted myself off and went back to try again.

The summit was a dream, but when I was climbing, I was as wide awake, as alert, as open to experience, as I've ever been in my life. Everest is behind me now, but I can still see the shadow of the mountain in everything I do. It's a reminder, and a challenge, from the highest spot on the world.

Look beyond the ordinary. There's always something more. As long as I remember that, I know anything is possible.

About the Author

Stacy Allison is a popular speaker who offers her powerful motivational presentations to audiences ranging from corporate executives to schoolchildren. She presents more than 50 talks each year to groups of 50 to 3,000 people.

Stacy's mission is to encourage people to move beyond their self-imposed limitations to reach for their dreams. She challenges her audiences to lay a foundation for risk-taking by accepting full responsibility for their choices and urges them to value their own and others' roles as team members in life's endeavors.

Beyond the Limits: A Woman's Triumph on Everest, Stacy's first book, is a suspenseful, triumphant adventure story—a primer for anyone who has ever faced a mountain, physical or metaphorical, and reached for its summit.

In addition to speaking, Stacy owns and operates Stacy Allison General Contracting, a residential building company specializing in the restoration and remodeling of older homes. She lives in Portland, Oregon, with her husband, David, a physician, and their two young sons.

Whether climbing mountains, building, speaking, or meeting the challenges of parenthood, Stacy is known for the energy, commitment, and conviction she brings to all her pursuits.

Take your next meeting to new heights!
To book Stacy Allison to speak at your event, contact her at:

7003 S.E. Reed College Place
Portland, Oregon 97202
Telephone: (503) 777-4023 Fax: (503) 788-9407
e-mail: Stacy@BeyondTheLimits.com
URL: http://www.beyondthelimits.com/speaks

Stacy Allison on the summit of Mt. Everest, 1988.

To order additional copies of

Many Mountains to Climb

Book: $15.95   Shipping/Handling: $3.50

Contact: **_BookPartners, Inc._**
P.O. Box 922
Wilsonville, OR 97070

E-mail: bpbooks@teleport.com
Fax: 503-682-8684
Phone: 503-682-9821
Order: 1-800-895-7323